Authority, Leadership
and Conflict in the Church

Authority, Leadership and Conflict in the Church

PAUL AVIS

Trinity Press International

Trinity Press International
3725 Chestnut Street, Philadelphia, Pennsylvania 19104, USA

First published 1992
Published in Great Britain by Mowbray, a Cassell imprint

Library of Congress Cataloging-in-Publication Data
Avis. Paul D. L.
Authority, leadership, and conflict in the church / Paul Avis.
p. cm.
Includes bibliographical references and index.
ISBN 1-56338-035-8 (pbk)
1. Church—Authority.   2. Christian leadership.   3. Church
controversies.   4. Church of England—Doctrines.   5. Anglican
Communion—Doctrines.   I. Title.
BT91.A85   1992
262'.03—dc20   91–43793
                                                             CIP

Typeset by Colset Private Limited, Singapore
Printed and bound in Great Britain by
Biddles Ltd, Guildford and King's Lynn

Contents

Foreword

by the Archbishop of York

Paul Avis first caught my eye in a perceptive critique of the ARCIC report on Authority published in *Theology* in 1983. Since then the theme of authority has seldom been far from his thoughts. He has pursued it from a variety of perspectives in a series of learned and impressive books, to which this latest addition is a worthy successor. Like the best Anglican theology it comes out of a country vicarage, and manages to be both critical and constructive, as well as firmly rooted in actual practice. It begins, for instance, with the Archbishop of Canterbury, and ends with a defence of stipend differentials. In between there is an instructive journey through psychology, sociology, group dynamics, management studies and much else, all informed by an acute theological awareness.

It could hardly be more topical. Adrian Hastings saw the main theme of Archbishop Runcie's primacy as the search for an appropriate Anglican style of authority. Avis himself wrote in 1986, 'Dissatisfaction with the Church of England centres on the question of authority'. The lust for infallible authorities seems to grow rather than be outgrown. And it is not only in Anglicanism, or the churches in general, that authority questions are of vital contemporary importance. I write this at a time when the authority structure of the Soviet Union seems to be crumbling, and our country is engaged in bloody conflict in the Gulf against yet another dictator.

The book is full of wise and well-grounded advice, not all of which will be popular. The requirement that leaders should have intellectual stature, for instance, will not please those who glory in Anglican amateurism. The description of authoritarianism as

vii

sado-masochistic throws a sharp light on the collusion between leaders and led in hierarchical systems. There are the expected criticisms of bureaucratic management as one extreme model for the Church, and 'signs and wonders' leadership as its equally inappropriate counterpoint. We are reminded of the need for openness to criticism and the harnessing of conflict, in a religious context which is now ineradicably pluralist.

Bearing in mind all this, the crunch question is whether the Church of England—and still more the Anglican Communion—is leadable. Not in the way some people want. But the cheering message of this book is that an appropriate style of leadership is not only possible, but necessary and Christian. And the better it works, the less likely people are to talk about it.

JOHN EBOR:

Preface

Authority has vanished from the modern world, it is claimed. But the churches still assume authority. Anglicanism believes that it embodies a dispersed authority that is compatible with much diversity of belief and practice. Roman Catholicism still asserts a plenary authority over the faith and morals of the faithful, and the Pope claims immediate universal jurisdiction over the Christian Church.

The popular cry is for unequivocal pronouncements from Canterbury—provided they are the ones with which the speaker happens to agree! The Pope is frequently pronouncing—but how seriously are his instructions taken by lay Catholics? Recent research suggests that they are largely ignored, especially in private matters. Are Church leaders now placed in an impossible position? Is religious authority a sustainable role any more? What forms of leadership are appropriate in our semi-secularized society? Given the pathological thirst for authority that has been such a disturbing feature of twentieth-century mass society, how can necessary leadership be exercised without creating unhealthy dependence?

The title of this book, though prosaic, effectively sums up its contents: *Authority, Leadership and Conflict in the Church*. In it I attempt to set up a dialogue between biblical and theological views of authority, on the one hand, and what the social sciences and management studies can teach us on the other. The conclusions I draw for the life and ministry of the Church today will not be welcomed by all. They are, to say the least, contestable. But I hope that the clear assertions of my argument—especially in the last three chapters—will stimulate the sort of serious discussion that the themes of authority, leadership and conflict deserve.

In sifting the available cross-disciplinary material for exploring the nature of authority, the anatomy of leadership and the dynamics of conflict, I trust that I have been able to present in serviceable form ample resources for the study of these topics in theological education.

In this book I am wrestling with the three specific themes of liberating authority, therapeutic leadership and constructive conflict:

LIBERATING AUTHORITY

A concept of authority that brings out its root meaning of enabling rather than dominating, and finds its justification in a spiritual and theological competence that invites voluntary acknowledgement rather than in hierarchical or bureaucratic demands for acquiescence.

THERAPEUTIC LEADERSHIP

A notion of leadership that transcends mere management—the efficient control and deployment of resources—and one which, instead of feeding on people's dependence and thus depotentiating them, gives back immature dependence and enables individuals and groups to take responsibility for themselves while being sustained and affirmed by a leadership that has not abdicated its own responsibilities.

CONSTRUCTIVE CONFLICT

An interpretation of conflict that, while not actively promoting it, suggests how conflict and argument, which are endemic in the Church, as in any living movement, may be channelled to benefit the enterprise rather than merely contained by managerial techniques.

I am encouraged to find that I seem to be in tune with recent Anglican thinking on ministry. In my book I have stressed that leadership demands outstanding intellectual ability and application and I have argued that inter-personal skills, though vital, are not sufficient qualification in themselves. The ACCM Occasional Paper 12, 'Selection for Ministry: A report on Criteria', published in 1983 and reissued in 1990, reminds us that the Church's ministers will increasingly be involved in the education and training of informed and articulate lay people, where prophetic and interpretative ministry is required in relating scripture and tradition to the modern world. The report concludes that the Church will need individuals of an increasingly high calibre in its professional ministry, endowed with intellectual vigour and vitality, alertness and imagination, as well as sensitivity and openness. While these qualities must not be detached from proficiency in prayer, there is a need for standards to rise (Advisory Council for the Church's Ministry, 1983, pp. 32ff.).

I have also emphasized that learning for leadership must be a lifelong process of development and enrichment, for leaders must never cease to be learners. ACCM Occasional Paper 22 (1987) points out that the knowledge and skills acquired or deepened in training must develop continuously as they are used in the service of the Church. Theological education is 'a lifelong process of personal development' for which pre-ordination training serves as the initial phase when important patterns are established (Advisory Council for the Church's Ministry, 1987, p. 34). This brings home the need to give priority to post-ordination training, in-service training and methods of ministerial development or assessment (about which I have something to say).

Using Weber's typology of traditional, bureaucratic and charismatic forms of authority, each with its distinctive kind of legitimation, I have stressed the need to understand the nature of the institutions in which we work. I have indicated, with the help of Weber's concept of 'the routinization of charisma', that we cannot opt out of these human, social and even worldly structures in the name of the freedom of the spirit. A recent ACCM working party on 'Ordination and the Church's Ministry' observed that Anglican colleges and courses frequently gave little attention to the Church as an institution, often presenting the mission of the Church purely in relation to the Kingdom of God—'as though the Kingdom was detachable from the Church's current practical engagement as a visible, structured body in the world'. Theological training, the report insists, 'has a responsibility to prepare ordinands for the Church of England as it is' (Advisory Council for the Church's Ministry, 1990, pp. 12ff.).

Using Ian Bunting's recent survey of theological education in Britain, and other sources, I have pointed to the low profile that the notion of leadership currently receives in training. The same ACCM document notes that some colleges and courses deploy 'an unexamined concept of leadership' as a substitute for a developed theology of ordained ministry. Vague notions of leadership offer a pragmatic working notion of ordained ministry which may be attractive because it enables difficult and sometimes unresolved doctrinal issues to be suspended (1990, p. 43). Needless to say, I do not present the concept of leadership as a substitute for theology of ordained ministry (which I have attempted in the chapter entitled 'Ministries in communion?' in my recent book *Christians in Communion*). My aim is to scrutinize the concepts of leadership and management and to ask to what extent they are applicable to a body such as the Church, which has a fundamentally sacred *raison d'être* and is made up of volunteers (lay people) and staffed by vocational officers (clergy). The methods of the social sciences do not pretend to plumb the theological rationale for the Christian Church and its ordained ministry, but they are perfectly well equipped to handle the notions of the sacred and of voluntary societies on a comparative basis.

It is a matter of regret to me that I have not been able to discuss the House Church movement—a flourishing example of that unreconstructed authority that Hannah Arendt claimed had vanished from the modern world! This recent phenomenon is only now beginning to be studied and Andrew Walker's *Restoring the Kingdom* is our starting point.

I am most grateful to those individuals who have given of their experience, insight and professional expertise in offering practical assistance or detailed comment on part or all of the text: Susan Avis, Grace Davie, Vanessa Parffrey, Brian Russell, John Saxbee and Joy Thompson. If I have stuck to my guns in declining to accept all of the generous advice my friends have imparted, on my own head be it!

I also thank Gillian Piper, my secretary, who has produced the final text of this study from my well-worn drafts with her customary efficiency and dedication.

I am indebted to His Grace the Archbishop of York, Dr John

Habgood, for his encouraging Foreword, which began life as the publisher's reader's report.

PAUL AVIS
Stoke Canon Vicarage
Exeter
England

4 April 1991

1
Leadership and Authority in Today's Church

ANGLICANISM: A VACUUM OF AUTHORITY?

A recent correspondent to *The Times*, deploring the decline of morals and family values, ended her letter with the *cri de coeur*, 'Where, O where, is the Archbishop of Canterbury?'

I take the lady's point: morals and family life are traditionally the Church's department—to be inculcated by precept, persuasion and example. It shows a sad decline when they have to be legislated for. But I also appreciate the dilemma faced by Church leaders. It would be easy for them to utter bland platitudes about traditional values, the integrity of the family, the sacredness of sex, and so on—and perhaps it is sometimes necessary for these to be uttered! But it is probably now impossible for a Church leader to give firm and unequivocal leadership in the area of ethical choices affecting sexual morality, for it is here above all that the frailty of human nature, the brittle fabric of modern society and the pluralism of contemporary values are most apparent.

The Church's message in this complex area of ethical dilemmas tends not to be in the form of laying down hard-and-fast rules, but rather in the form of supporting those who, on the whole, are managing to live up to their moral ideals, comforting those whose lives may be in a tangle, and counselling those who come seeking advice in the face of moral problems.

That, at least, would appear to be the Anglican approach. Its notion of authority is somewhat attenuated. It seeks guidance from

1

many sources. It encourages the individual to think and decide for himself or herself. It fears to intrude on the sanctity of conscience. Its character is personal and pastoral rather than legal and formal.

But it is capable of another interpretation. It has been unkindly said that, in the matter of sexual behaviour, Anglican bishops refuse to say anything that could not be said by a secular, tabloid agony aunt (Lee and Stanford, p. 65)—though now an exception must be made for the admirable statement by the Church of England House of Bishops, *Issues in Human Sexuality* (1991). A 'hermeneutic of suspicion' might ask whether the Anglican way pointed not so much to moral delicacy and a sense of the intractability of modern problems, as to lack of rigour in theology—especially moral theology—and of the courage to take unpleasant decisions. It is sometimes suggested that, while *leadership* is about *solving* problems, *management* is concerned with *containing* problems. To the extent that this is true—and later chapters will examine the distinction between leadership and management—it suggests that the Anglican approach shies away from leadership and leans instead towards management. But mere management, without articulating a moral vision, setting out goals for activity and standards of performance, would be an abdication of the responsibilities that belongs to the office of a bishop or archbishop. Certainly many contemporary commentators have discerned a *vacuum of authority* in Anglicanism. Anglicanism stands in need of a strengthening of its authority in several respects.

First, Anglicanism needs the authority *to know itself for what it is*. Anglicanism is seeking to rediscover its identity and its heritage of theology and spirituality as a branch of the Church Catholic. It is beginning to explore the meaning of 'communion' between provinces and between various traditions of churchmanship. It is attempting to engage more confidently in ecumenical dialogue and fellowship with a strong sense of what it stands for and what it has to offer. Anglicanism needs the authority imparted by self-knowledge (cf. Avis, 1989a).

Secondly, Anglicanism needs the authority *to know what its ministry is*. Is it the ministry of the Body of Christ into which all Christians have been incorporated by baptism? Is it a ministry that is representative of the whole Body and acceptable to the whole Body? Is it a ministry that reflects the royal priesthood of the Church which all men and women share by baptism, reflecting it back to the whole community so that it may exercise its own priesthood more effectively? To be specific, Anglicanism needs to know that it has the authority to ordain women to its ministry (cf. Avis, 1990, ch. 6).

Thirdly, Anglicanism needs the authority *to know what its gospel is*. In an age of chronic religious pluralism, and amid the competing claims of other religions and ideologies, it needs to know what claims for Christianity can still be made with confidence. In the light of the social sciences' critique of religion and of modern biblical scholarship, it needs the authority to be able to say, 'This we believe' and 'This we preach'.

ROMAN CATHOLICISM:
AN EXCESS OF AUTHORITY?

If, however, we are looking for strong leadership, for hard-and-fast rules to live by, for firm prohibitions, while the Anglican episcopate may be somewhat reticent, the Vatican has no such inhibitions. The Church of Rome—and specifically the present Pope—offers authority and leadership. There will always be a market for that.

In the Roman Catholic understanding, the Church enjoys the fullness of God-given authority to rule its members—to prescribe what they shall believe and how they shall live. Christ acts through the Church—and the Church, in turn, acts corporately through the Pope, the successor of Peter. The Pope contains in his office all the power of the Church, which would continue to subsist in him even if the whole body of the faithful were to be wiped out. The Roman Catholic Church is a monarchy, a hierarchically structured society, with the Pope at the apex of the pyramid. Attempts at the Second Vatican Council to introduce elements of a constitutional monarchy, by placing the Pope at the head of the college of bishops, were undermined in the new canon law. Papal authority remains absolute (Archer, pp. 7f., 147f.).

The Church speaks with the voice of Christ. Christ did not err, so the Church does not teach error. However, the divine gift of inerrancy is tied to being in accord with the Pope. Dissent, even on grounds of conscience, is a rejection of the voice of Christ. The Church's tradition transmits in its entirety the Word of God entrusted by Christ and the Holy Spirit to the apostles and thence to their successors, the bishops in communion with the See of Rome. The content is unchanging though the presentation develops (as Pope John XXIII stated with such strategic significance at the opening of the Second Vatican Council). However, only the official, central teaching office of the Church (the Magisterium) enjoys the gift of discerning authentic development, so any theologian who thinks that he (or she) has discovered a new insight—one that contradicts official teaching—knows that they must be mistaken.

The Pope has a God-given mission to the whole world, and especially to all the baptized, 'whether they will hear or whether they will forbear'. Rome has always claimed jurisdiction over all other Churches and she is not about to trade in that fundamental claim for the sake of ecumenical goodwill. The Church insists on these prerogatives not out of pride and self-aggrandizement, but because it loves us and wills only the best for us.

The Pope's ethical teaching is a prime example of unabashed authority. There are no grey areas: the two-edged sword of papal authority divides unerringly between right and wrong. The rights of unborn children are valiantly upheld. But contraception, including vasectomy, is condemned as the instrument of selfish sexual gratification without responsibility—an attack on the person and therefore on the body. Surrogate motherhood is on the same level as prostitution. Homosexual activity cannot, a priori, be a form of mutual self-giving. Premarital sex is placed on the same level as adultery—both are ways of using another person for selfish ends. Artificial insemination—even for childless couples—treats the body as a mechanism and the resulting child as an industrial product.

These are not the paranoid anti-Roman fantasies of an Anglican liberal—though Roman Catholic apologists will no doubt be quick to brand this picture as a caricature and to assure us that the Roman Church does not feel like that from the inside. These statements are taken from a recent factual account of the teaching of Pope John Paul II, bearing the Imprimatur (Hogan and Le Voir).

Rome represents a last manifestation of the centralized authoritarian régime now that so many such régimes have toppled in Eastern Europe. It embodies the ideal that many Communist states so signally failed to realize, undermined and destroyed by corruption and inefficiency as they were. Rome believes in controlling the faithful for their own good. Many observers, both inside and outside the Roman Catholic Church, regard it as suffering from *an excess of authority*.

Vatican II warned against assuming that the Church has all the answers. 'Let the layman not imagine that his pastors are always such experts, that to every problem which arises, however complicated, they can readily give him a concrete solution; or even that such is their mission' (Abbott (ed.), p. 244). Bruno Brinkman has warned against the notion of the omnicompetent Church: 'The Church in its faith is not a spiritual variant of a welfare-state-cum-consumer-society. . . . Clarity, tangibility, effulgent presence . . . are by no means signs of a deeper faith. . . . Creeping infallibility is also an infidelity to the grace of God's primary witness' (pp. 27f.). Autocracy is not the same as leadership. Compliance is not the authentic response that we offer to true leaders.

If Anglicanism needs a strengthening of its authority, to fill the vacuum of authority, the Roman Catholic Church stands in need of a renunciation of authority, a critical deconstruction of its self-understanding as far as authority is concerned. The excess of authority from which it suffers at the present time appears to be hindering that communion's development in several areas.

First, Rome needs to lose authority in order *to enter without reserve into the ecumenical process*, which is a journey of mutual understanding in the context of mutual unreserved acceptance. While Roman Catholics are not allowed to receive holy communion from other Christian churches—even though their members are recognized as Christians, baptized into Christ's Body and sharing in his threefold messianic office as prophets, priests and kings—and while members of other churches, though so recognized, are not allowed to receive holy communion from the Roman Catholic Church (even though their understanding of what is being offered and received is undeniably far superior to that of the small children communicated by Rome—or even of the disciples at the Last Supper!), that unreserved mutual acceptance cannot be said to exist. What interpretation can Anglicans, for example, place on this policy, other than that Rome is still licking the wounds of the Reformation, and that when the Roman hierarchy defends this policy as 'the price of separation' it really means 'a punishment for schism' (cf. Avis, 1990)?

Secondly, Rome needs to shed authority in order *to liberate the theological, liturgical and pastoral potential* of the young churches of the developing world, especially in South America, the Far East and Africa, so that they may find their own identity, develop a theology appropriate to their needs, and work out a pastoral strategy to meet their circumstances—even if that means a liberation theology with political involvement by the clergy, married priests and more spontaneity in the liturgy. As Karl Rahner suggested (pp. 86ff.)

(with tongue firmly in cheek, I suspect), the Sacred Congregation for the Doctrine of the Faith ought to open branches in various parts of the world so that the monitoring of theological views, etc. would be compelled to take account of local problems, circumstances and modes of thought. A strong centralized authority that insists on taking all important decisions itself (including the appointment of bishops) can only exist in a state of increasing tension with the plurality of Christian ecclesial forms that are developing today. As we have seen recently in Eastern Europe, national and local identities reasserting themselves come into conflict with centralized government. The central authority can only succeed in maintaining control while the system is believed to be working. When the system begins to break down—through inefficiency, corruption, lack of flexibility, lack of motivation—central authority is forced to slacken its grip: its credibility is lost for ever. So it is in the Roman Catholic communion worldwide: as soon as shortage of priests or of funds, disaffection from the institutional Church, and the 'spontaneous' creation of alternative communities begin to make their presence felt, authority begins to crumble. Ideological justification cannot long triumph over practical necessities. While Rome may be compelled to make a reluctant accommodation to the demands of local churches, how much better it would be if Rome were to acknowledge that a truly liberating authority—one that accepts the post-Enlightenment suspicion of all forms of imposed authority—is the best guardian of spiritual vitality in theology, and pastoral practice.

Thirdly, Rome needs to renounce authority in order *to meet one of the most fundamental challenges to the Christian faith—the feminist critique* of the patriarchal and androcentric nature of Christian theology and Church practice. It needs to strip off the authority that underlies claims that its teachings and practices are God-given and unchanging in order to take to heart the radical critique that, drawing on the insights of the social sciences, exposes such claims as nakedly ideological—as reflecting and defending certain social structures and group interests. It needs to shed the carapace of authoritarianism in order to heed what is now known about the formation of sexual identity, the real differences (other than those attributable to social conditioning) between women and men, and the 'androgynous' character of human wholeness. It needs the humility to reflect on how all this affects our picture of God and how we speak of God in theology and liturgy and how we portray the sacred in the world of religious symbolism. The deconstruction of patriarchy is the most searching challenge to Roman authoritarianism (Avis, 1989b).

GENERAL AND SPECIFIC AUTHORITY

Anglicanism and Roman Catholicism represent, then, two contrasting climates of authority, reflecting two opposing trends in Western cultural history. The appeal to authority and the thirst for freedom exist in tension in the modern world. Firm rule and decisive leadership (with their pathological accompaniments: paranoia and irrationality, blind fanaticism and the idolization of leaders), on the one hand, and the spirit of liberty, the quest for autonomy, the freedoms of democratic civilization (with all their abuses and excesses!) on the other, have been pronounced in recent history. Which way is the Church to choose? Perhaps it wants to be pragmatic, giving people what they want: there is nothing new in this. Roman dogma has tended to respond to popular piety—as, for example, in the promulgation of the Marian dogmas. And in the Church of England, the House of Bishops has recently been intimidated, it would seem, into wishing to give the impression of being more conservative, more 'orthodox' than it really is (in the report *The Nature of Christian Belief*—a response to the Bishop of Durham's views and the controversy that they aroused). But if the Church wishes to take account of consumer preference, it will have to make up its mind which way to jump. It is quite likely to get it wrong! Michael Polanyi's distinction between general and specific authority is helpful here (pp. 43–5).

General authority, according to Polanyi, does not attempt to specify detailed programmes or conclusions, but is concerned with fostering the appropriate presuppositions that individuals are then free to follow in the light of conscience. This is the method of science, of law, and of Protestant (including Anglican) theology. Like science, theology explores a given reality, that of the sacred, with its complex of divine revelation and human interpretation that are only distinguishable conceptually and not empirically. Like law, theology attempts to respond to unfamiliar, even unprecedented, circumstances, and to apply the tradition creatively to every fresh problem. Polanyi writes:

> A General Authority relies for the initiative in the gradual transformation of tradition on the intuitive impulses of the

7

individual adherents of the community and it relies on their consciences to control their intuitions. The General Authority itself is but a more or less organized expression of the general opinion—scientific, legal or religious—formed by the merging and interplay of all these individual contributions. Such a regime assumes that individual members are capable of making a genuine contact with the reality underlying the existing tradition and of adding new and authoritative interpretations to it.

Polanyi's conception of *dispersed* authority has a close affinity with the Anglican self-understanding: 'Innovation in this case is done at numerous growing points dispersed through the community, each of which may take the lead over the whole at any particular moment.'

Specific authority, on the other hand, lays down detailed policies, programmes or conclusions to be followed. In contrast to general authority, which fosters creative freedom with its attendant risks, specific authority requires obedience because it believes that the answers are already in its possession and simply need to be accepted and implemented. In place of exploration of a reality that forever transcends our grasp, it offers the defence and refinement of received wisdom. Response to fresh challenges and unprecedented situations will be prescribed by those who are not immediately involved and will generally take the form of reaffirming traditional teaching. Polanyi writes:

> A Specific Authority . . . makes all important reinterpretations and innovations by pronouncements from the centre. This centre alone is thought to have authoritative contacts with the fundamental sources from which the existing tradition springs and can be renewed. Specific Authority demands therefore not only devotion to the tenets of a tradition but subordination of everyone's ultimate judgement to the discretionary decision by an official centre.

Polanyi explicitly has the Roman Catholic Church in mind, but the same description fits all centralized authoritarian structures. Polanyi's diagnosis explains why the Kremlin has lost its empire and why Hitler lost the war.

THE POWER-BASE OF CHURCH AUTHORITY

No authority exists in a vacuum. All forms of authority find their *raison d'être* in the context of a particular community and in relation to the specific goals of that community. In other words, all authority has its own power-base. As Margaret Thatcher discovered, you take that power-base for granted at your peril! David Watt has written:

> Authority, in all its forms, is found only where a number of people are gathered together in some activity which depends upon their several roles. It is by reference to some activity that every instance of authority may be understood, and where justification is needed, justified. The limits of any authority are likewise understood by reference to the activity within which it operates. (Watt, p. 105)

How does this analysis apply to the authority of Church leaders?

(a) THE AUTHORITY OF CHURCH LEADERS IS LOCATED WITHIN THE CHRISTIAN COMMUNITY

Though this may seem to be stating the obvious, the implications are not always drawn from it. Bishops and archbishops of a territorial Church—though they may have a national and even international role to play—have their primary power-base in the parishes—a power-base that requires cultivating. They should therefore speak for—and to—ordinary Church people, the rank and file of the Church, those who keep the Church's worship and witness going week by week: the members of Church Councils and Vestries, the sidespersons, flower arrangers, lesson-readers and choristers in parish churches up and down the land. It must be possible for ordinary church members to identify with their leaders and to sense that their leaders identify with them. The morale of lay folk in the parishes is raised by leaders who by word and deed affirm the value of the everyday parish-based way of being a Christian.

Since the power-base of leaders of the Church is parochial and not eclectic or free-standing, leaders diminish their own power-base when they give succour to sectarian notions of the Church. The parochial consciousness is largely one without hard edges: in the parishes, the Church is compelled to keep its borders open. Church leaders should throw their weight, by example and precept, against the drift towards a merely sectarian identity for the Church. They should endeavour to hold the clergy to their pastoral obligations to all their parishioners, especially through the ministry of the so-called occasional offices—baptism, matrimony and burial.

However, the Archbishop of Canterbury's power-base extends to the whole Anglican Communion. The 1988 Lambeth Conference showed very strikingly how, as Archbishop Robert Runcie welcomed the bishops from the four corners of the earth with his incomparable warmth and humanity, they in turn affirmed him in his office as president of the Communion. An Archbishop of Canterbury therefore needs to be persuaded of the value and potential of the Anglican Communion as an estimable expression of a reformed catholicism and as an experiment in communion between churches that enjoy provincial integrity. An archbishop sceptical of the value of the Communion simply because its bonds and constraints are tacit and personal rather than canonical and political, or an archbishop over-awed by a romantic reading of the jurisdictional and magisterial structures of the Roman Catholic Church, would be disastrous for Anglicanism at a time when it is beginning to find its identity and to explore the structures of primacy (consultation of primates and the role of the Archbishop of Canterbury), collegiality (collective responsibility) and conciliarity (the authority of the Church in Council—highly problematical though that is in the modern pluralistic context).

(b) THE AUTHORITY OF CHURCH LEADERS IS RELATED TO THE COMMON GOALS OF THE CHRISTIAN COMMUNITY

Authority exists, not in isolation, or to perpetuate itself, but purely to advance the aims of the community—to prosecute the task. The primary task of any institution is what it must achieve to ensure its survival. Since no institution is entirely self-contained, but instead is open to its environment, that task is a function of its environment as well as of its internal character. It must therefore provide a 'pay-off' for the environment and for the enterprise itself. Its activities must serve to relate the members of the institution to its reciprocating environment. These activities—the activities that put the overall task into effect—should take account both of conscious policy aims and of unconscious emotional demands (Reed, p. 146). The task of the Church, therefore, will have both explicit and tacit aspects, those that are verbally articulated and those that are symbolically expressed.

As far as servicing the identity of the Christian community itself is concerned, we have already emphasized the requirement to cultivate the power-base by affirming the members in their lay vocations and in their diverse contributions to the ongoing life of the parish. But the identity and cohesion of the community must not be bought at the expense of openness to the environment. A closed Church is a Church doomed to extinction. It should be possible to motivate Christian people to find their common God-given cause in the service of those who are not yet themselves members and to see this as their primary task. The survival of the Church depends on the existence of sufficient points of contact, entry and attachment for those coming within the Church's sphere of influence. Strategy should therefore be directed towards maximizing those points of contact, entry and attachment. This is of course done through the Church's educational, social and aesthetic (architecture, music, flowers and 'the beauty of holiness') ministry, as well as by means of the occasional offices. For it is those on the periphery of the Church, those whose lives have already been touched by it at some point, who form the pool from which most new members are drawn.

The cohesion of the community and the coherence of the strategy it pursues in furtherance of this task depends on each member having a sense of common purpose. Though the identity and goals of the Church—like those of any other community with aims that, in the nature of the case, transcend the immediate selfish gratification of the individuals who comprise it—are articulated symbolically, through ritual and especially sacrament, they need also to be brought to consciousness, so that participants have a sense of being valued and needed for the prosecution of the common task. This exercise is the corporate clarification of goals. Lasswell has written:

> The principle of clarification takes into account the undeniable though often neglected fact that men are conscious and can be rational. Human beings resent being left in the dark about the ends of an enterprise in which they are engaged. The act of affirming or admitting a common goal is enough in itself to release human energies to an astounding extent. (1949, p. 188)

Lasswell himself stresses the vital role of 'goal symbols that specify the direction and justification of collective action' (ibid.).

(c) THE AUTHORITY OF CHURCH LEADERS HAS A SYMBOLIC FUNCTION

In this symbolic process, priests, bishops and archbishops play a critical role. A priest, a bishop and an archbishop all stand for something before they open their mouths. So they need not be frequently uttering and should beware of the law of diminishing returns. They must be perceived to stand for eternal truths and values and so must be 'above the fray'. It would not do for a parish priest to be always quoting from spokesmen (or spokeswomen) for the latest theological fashion, or for bishops to be closely identified with the policies of a particular political party, or even for an archbishop to give his overt backing to particular and specific programmes of action. Rather, Christian leaders must be perceived to be (and indeed must actually be!) people of spiritual attainment and vision who take their orders from God—not from the General Synod, the Pope or the liberal consensus. Identification with programmes or strategies always alienates a significant constituency of people of goodwill who share the principles, but disagree about the most effective, just or compassionate way of putting them into practice.

The symbolic significance of Christian leaders is apparent in the fact that they do not have to have popular appeal. The common touch is not necessary for authority and can even diminish it. William Temple was called 'the people's archbishop', though he was a massively intellectual man born and bred within a very privileged environment. Cardinal Basil Hume has a moral authority that extends well beyond his own communion, although he appears shy and fastidious: he comes over as a man of spiritual strength who believes he knows what the will of God and the Church is, even though it may be unpopular.

(d) THE AUTHORITY OF CHURCH LEADERS IS CONSTRAINED BY THE
    ECUMENICAL ENVIRONMENT

Other Christian churches also constitute an aspect of the environment of a particular Church. It is, as always, a reciprocating environment, one that helps to shape the sense of identity—the place, role, function and boundary—of a Church. The ecumenical enterprise also requires points of contact, access and mutual affirmation, since churches no longer define themselves in a self-sufficient way, but in relation to the ideal of a future united Church. As a journey of deepening mutual understanding in the context of unconditional mutual acceptance, the ecumenical quest requires that churches should not pretend to be other than they really are (cf. Avis, 1990, ch. 1). For churches to be rewarding partners in this enterprise, they must pay attention to their evolving identity. They must be convinced that they have much to give, as well as much to gain— something to teach as well as something to learn—from the ecumenical exchange.

As far as Anglicanism is concerned, therefore, its leaders should claim the moral high ground. They should not appear as suppliants before more prestigious communions of the Christian Church, or allow themselves to be outmanoeuvred (as when Dr Robert Runcie was seen by millions kneeling on the sidelines while the Pope celebrated mass in St Peter's Square). They will not wish to be apologetic about the ecclesiological credentials of the Anglican Communion— its character as a Church that is both catholic and reformed and at the same time open to the contribution of 'sound learning'. Anglicans can take the moral high ground, for example, over intercommunion (their practice of eucharistic hospitality should put others to shame!) and over the ordination of women as priests and bishops (as an instance of the continual reformation of the Church).

AN AGENDA FOR LEADERSHIP

The task of the Church will only be achieved if it is able to offer a *vision of the human good* that is attractive and compelling to its own members and to people of goodwill outside the Church who are open to what it offers. This is a primary aspect of its moral leadership: to redefine and refocus the aims and values of the community. This vision of the good for humanity will have to be larger than the immediate imperatives to feed the hungry and house the homeless. The Church must have an answer to the question: What is God's purpose for our lives when the oppressed have been liberated? The dignity and sanctity of human life—that motivates what the Church says and does about the poor, the oppressed and the vulnerable in society—must be set in the broader context of the Christian perception of the wholeness and fullness of human life based on the doctrines of creation and redemption.

Popular spiritual concern, represented broadly by the phenomena encompassed in the so-called New Age movement, has two major dimensions: *ecological*, concerned with the protection of the environment against human industrial exploitation, and *therapeutic*, concerned with the healing and wholeness of the person in body, mind and spirit. These together imply a perception and valuation of nature—of the physical cosmos and of human nature—about which Christian theology has traditionally had little positive to say.

Furthermore, the vision of the human good requires an ethic of success. Human beings are only interested in being successful in all they do and in creating prosperity for themselves, their dependants and their successors. I would guess that the popular perception of the Church at the present time is that it is more interested in sanctifying failure than in promoting success. Nothing is more calculated to render the Church irrelevant! If recent developments in Eastern Europe, as well as trends in Western Europe, have demonstrated that state socialism does not bring success and prosperity, does that not suggest a role for the Church in developing an ethic of success? The Church will have to adjust to a new role as the conscience of capitalism if it wants a role at all.

Another major area for the attention of the churches is the question of sexuality and the sacred, where the Church has traditionally been negative or at least extremely diffident. But it belongs to the doctrine of creation to affirm the created sexuality of humans. Putting it bluntly, for two thousand years the Church has given the firm impression that it does not—that God does not—approve of sex! To be conscious of divine disapproval in one of the most pervasive and powerful dimensions of our humanity has cast a dark shadow of misery and guilt down the ages. It has been justly claimed that in the area of human sexuality the Church has consistently failed humankind.

Since in the patriarchal culture that is only now beginning to be superseded, women have been made the repositories of the negative emotions that that attitude generates, and their personhood has been concealed and defaced by destructive projections which have rendered them 'icons of the erotic', the Church has a massive task of repentant rethinking and practical reparation thrust upon it. No one will believe the Church's belated assurances that sexuality is a God-given endowment to be used for human happiness and fulfilment and for the divine glory, until the whole Church shows in decisive practical action that it neither regards sexuality as suspect nor identifies women as icons of the erotic, by ordaining them to holy tasks (the sacramental ministry) in a holy place (the sanctuary) (cf. Avis, 1989b).

At the same time, it will not do for the Church to take a simplistic celebratory or liberationist attitude to human sexuality. It would be

14

an abnegation of theological and pastoral responsibility to encourage mere self-expression. The Church is called to that hardest of intellectual tasks—discrimination. If it cannot offer—and insist upon—firm but compassionate life-rules, disciplines, boundaries for sexual behaviour, the last state will be worse than the first. The Church cannot afford to be perceived to stand for mere benevolent platitudes, but must develop concrete proposals—régimes for handling the boundary situations of sexuality—that neither demand the impossible (e.g. total celibacy for homosexuals) nor undermine all that the Church is striving to inculcate in relation to the great majority of its constituency through the marriage and baptism liturgies—for example, by ordaining active homosexuals 'on demand' (Avis, 1989b, ch. 17).

These issues that now confront the Church's leadership demand theological judgement based on extensive resources of information and an insight that is both delicate and profound. There are questions here to occupy theologians in the areas of creation, theological anthropology and Christian ethics and to generate a massive programme of clerical and lay education. What price authority as competence today?

2

The Power and the Glory

Few individuals have exercised such power in a succession of political offices over half a century or been accorded such glory in the grateful estimation of so many people throughout the world as Sir Winston Churchill. But Churchill knew what it was to have power snatched from him, as in the election of 1945 and the wilderness decade of the 1930s. And he had had first-hand experience of the ephemerality and fickleness of human glory. Empire after empire had crashed in ruins during his lifetime, kings had been toppled from their thrones, all-powerful dictators had been crushed. Churchill himself had on several occasions been compelled to exchange the trappings of power and popularity for the frustration and humiliation of political exile.

Two months after Churchill had reluctantly relinquished the premiership for the second time, in 1955, his son Randolph wrote to console him as he entered the twilight of old age:

> Power must pass and vanish. Glory, which is achieved through a just exercise of power—which itself is accumulated by genius, toil, courage and self-sacrifice—alone remains. Your glory is enshrined forever on the imperishable plinth of your achievement; and can never be destroyed or tarnished. It will flow with the centuries. (Gilbert, pp. 1160, 1366)

It is one of the supreme ironies of Christianity that, while in its daily prayer it ascribes 'the power and the glory' to God alone, it is itself deeply implicated in the pursuit, the retention and the exercise of power, and its leaders have not been averse to a share of the glory. In its battle for the hearts and minds of humanity the Church is

16

pitted against other ideologies—secularism, hedonism, atheistic materialism and other militant faiths—in a power struggle. As a human and social institution, the Christian Church cannot be exempt from the law that all social activity involves the distribution of power.

Niccolò Machiavelli (1469–1527) was possibly the first to define the 'ethics' of power. Bacon praised him for describing human nature as it is, rather than as it ought to be. For Machiavelli, what drives humanity is *necessità*. Human actions are spurred by the struggle for survival—by hunger, poverty and fear—on the one hand, and by ambition and avarice—'love of power' and 'love of substance'—on the other. In his history of Florence, Machiavelli makes Cosimo the Old say that 'men do not rule states with paternosters in their hands'. They do not rule the Church thus either! Croce said of Machiavelli that he had shown that human affairs are governed by the inexorable laws of political necessity which cannot be exorcized from this world by holy water (for references see Avis, 1986b, pp. 36ff.).

Thomas Hobbes (1588–1679) intensified, if anything, Machiavelli's cynical vision in his *Leviathan*. Human desire is insatiable and to live is to lust for gratification. 'The felicity of this life consisteth not in the repose of a mind satisfied. . . . Nor can a man any more live, whose desires are at an end, than he whose senses and imaginations are at a stand. Felicity is a continual progress of the desire, from one object to another' (Hobbes, 1962, p. 122). Of all human desires, the most fundamental—and elemental—is the lust for power, born of fear and generating fear in others. 'I put for a general inclination of all mankind, a perpetual and restless desire of power after power, that ceaseth only in death.' Those who possess power can only preserve what they have by acquiring more (pp. 122f.; cf. Avis, 1986b, pp. 95ff.).

Bertrand Russell's *Power* (1938) displays a Hobbesian vision of human motivation, albeit somewhat nuanced. Once basic survival needs have been satisfied, imagination goads human beings into restless exertion to fulfil their 'insatiable and infinite' desires. Of these infinite desires, the chief are the desires for power and glory. Though not identical, these are closely connected. The British Prime Minister has more power than the Queen, but the Queen has greater glory than her Prime Minister. But as a rule, the easiest way to obtain glory is to obtain power. The desire for glory tends to prompt the same courses of action as the desire for power, so 'the two motives

17

may, for most practical purposes, be regarded as one'. Russell claims that power was the fundamental concept of social science, more basic than economic self-interest, since the desire for material commodities, when separated from power and glory, is limited or finite and subject to the law of diminishing returns, but the desire for power and glory, quite apart from material gratification, is infinite. Wealth, like armed strength, civil authority and influence on opinion, is one form of power. Russell acknowledges that love of power is very unevenly distributed among human beings and is moderated by other motives, such as indolence, sensuous pleasure and desire for the approval of others. Furthermore, 'it is disguised, among the more timid, as an impulse of submission to leadership, which increases the scope of the power-impulses of bold men', wrote Russell in the late 1930s (pp. 8–13).

Machiavelli, Hobbes and Russell constitute weighty testimony to the centrality of power in human affairs. But someone might protest that this analysis does not do justice to the Christian Church, which claims to be moved by higher motives than the quest for power—by compassion for suffering humanity, by love 'of the brethren', by desire for the glory of God alone, by concern for the eternal welfare of individuals. It is true that the Church no longer exercises power in the form of physical coercion, as do the armed forces and the police, nor does it offer material inducements to extend its sway—though it is not long since material rewards were part and parcel of missionary tactics. It does, however, hold out the promise of ultimate spiritual reward, if not for this life, then for the life to come, and in that sense does certainly offer incentives to individuals to accept its régime. But above all, the Church exercises influence over the lives and minds of its members and seeks to extend that influence by persuasion of those outside. That sort of sway must be deemed a form of power. It brings the Church within the orbit of power-structures and power-play and renders it subject to power-analysis. The Church claims authority, and authority—even moral authority—is a mode of power. This in itself exposes the Church to a critique of power—indeed, it requires the Church to undertake that critique for itself. In his trenchant study of the exercise of authority in the New Testament, Graham Shaw asks:

> Is all religious authority of its nature oppressive, evading criticism by divisive social attitudes? Is the Christian gospel inherently self-contradictory, promising freedom but enforcing

obedience, promising reconciliation but sanctioning division? Is the language of Christianity a device for disguising the exercise of power? (Shaw, p. 12)

Let us try to clarify the relation between power and authority by examining some definitions.

(a) The root meaning of the English word 'authority' is profoundly liberational and therapeutic. It stems from the Latin verb *augere*, to make increase, to cause to grow, to fertilize, to strengthen or enlarge. This gave the noun root *auctor*, a doer, causer, creator, founder, beginner or leader. The senses of enabling and nurturing are fundamental—*auctoritas* meaning weighty counsel: 'more than advice and less than command', as Watt puts it (Watt, p. 14). This enabling *auctoritas* is distinguished from *imperium*, order, command, power, mastery, government (for without *auctoritas*, *imperium* is mere coercion), and from *potentia*, naked power, and *potestas*, legal power (cf. Skinner in Sykes (ed.), pp. 34ff.; Hill, p. 16).

A comparable distinction between authority and power is found in classical and New Testament Greek. *Exousia* in classical Greek is the ability to perform an action to the extent that there are no obstacles in the way, and the right to do something granted by a higher authority. In the Greek Old Testament (LXX), *exousia* means right, authority or permission, the legal or political freedom to act. In the New Testament, as Foerster writes, it 'signifies the absolute possibility of action which is proper to God' (*TDNT*, II, p. 567), as in Luke 12.5 ('*exousia* to cast into *Gehenna*'). When applied to Jesus Christ it denotes his divinely given dominion and status (Matthew 28.18: 'All· *exousia* in heaven and on earth has been given to me'). *Exousia* is ultimately divine authority (Mark 2.10: 'the Son of man has *exousia* on earth to forgive sins'). *Exousia* is the right that lies behind the exercise of power (*dynamis*), though the two terms are sometimes used almost synonymously.

Dynamis is the effective expression of *exousia* (Grundmann in *TDNT*, II, p. 310). In classical Greek, *dynamis* is strength, might, power, ability. In the Synoptic gospels it denotes (i) *miraculous* power (Mark 5.30: 'aware that *dynamis* had gone forth from him'; Matthew 11.21, 23: 'deeds of power'); (ii) *eschatological* power (Mark 9.1: 'that the kingdom of God has come with power'; 13.26: 'coming . . . with great power and glory'); and (iii) the power of the *Holy Spirit* (Luke 4.14: 'Jesus, filled with the power of the Spirit'). Barrett defines *dynamis* as 'the power of God in action, force doing work . . . kinetic energy' (1966, p. 78).

In the New Testament it is *exousia* that legitimates *dynamis*. Mere dynamic phenomena are not spiritually significant or theologically valid. The *exousia* of God and his Christ are not enforced by dynamic coercion, except in some eschatological scenarios, but are open to being freely acknowledged and willingly obeyed. The temptation for the Christian Church, as an institution, as an *imperium* even, has always been to take the short cut to mere power and to forget that the true substance of power, without which it is bankrupt and discredited, is the *exousia*, the 'moral authority' that it receives from God through the Christ whose authority did not prevent him being nailed to a cross. As early as Jerome's Latin New Testament (Vulgate), we find the Greek *exousia* being translated by the Latin *potestas* (legal power) rather than *auctoritas* (authority), as in Matthew 7.29: (Latin: 'he taught as one having power over them'; cf. Mark 11.28–33). The Church has power even now: power to make human beings happy or wretched, power to manipulate consciences and to play upon emotions, power to foster human potential, dignity and freedom or to stifle it. But does it have true authority—the moral authority and the authority of competence in the things of the spirit—that can afford to be open, frank and fair in all its dealings with its members and with the world outside? The tension between *auctoritas* and *potestas* or *imperium*, between *exousia* and *dynamis*, will continue to exercise us throughout this book.

(b) Russell defined power as 'the production of intended effects' (B. Russell, p. 35).

Dennis H. Wrong, in one of the most substantial treatments of power of recent years, has defined power, following Russell, as 'the capacity of some persons to produce intended and foreseen effects on others' (Wrong, p. 2). This need not be taken in a hierarchical or unilateral sense, for relations of power within a social nexus are often reciprocating—one party exercising power towards another in one area, and the other party enjoying power towards the first party in another area (p. 11). Wrong's definition, in terms of an intentional effect on others, can be taken in a trivial sense, for we inevitably influence everyone whose path crosses ours. Wrong recognizes a spectrum of modes of power from coercion at one extreme, through manipulation or persuasion by means of arguments, appeals and exhortations, to 'authority' at the other (p. 21).

What does Wrong mean by authority? Clearly it is the antithesis of coercion and does not need to employ manipulative methods or persuasive skills. The essence of authority is the power to issue commands that are complied with and complied with willingly. When the power-holder enjoys an acknowledged right to command and the power-subject has an acknowledged obligation to obey, we may speak of 'legitimate authority' (Wrong, pp. 35ff., 49).

(c) Other writers employ a narrower definition of power. Bierstedt defines power as the ability to use force—'the ability to employ force, not its actual employment, the ability to apply sanctions, not their actual application'. Bierstedt does not recognize persuasion or authority based on acknowledged competence as forms of power (Wrong, p. 21). Lasswell and Kaplan see influence as a form of power when it is backed by sanctions. 'Any form of influence may be regarded as in fact a power relation if the deprivations imposed by the influential are important enough to those over whom influence is being exercised' (Lasswell, 1949, p. 229). Those deprivations or sanctions may presumably be 'spiritual' ones in the case of the Church— exclusion from the sources of sacramental grace that can alone make us worthy of heaven. Weber called 'the distribution or denial of religious benefits' by the clergy 'hierocratic coercion' (Weber, p. 154). On this conception, moral influence is merely the kid glove concealing the iron fist. Dahrendorf has maintained that the possibility of imposing sanctions remains the 'abstract core of all power' (Ng, p. 81).

(d) Lukes has put forward a more sophisticated and ideologically suspicious interpretation of power, where it may be exercised effectively without obvious conflict. The most insidious form of power, according to Lukes, is where the power-holder influences, shapes and determines the wants and desires of the subject so that he complies willingly. People's perceptions, cognitions and preferences may be shaped in such a way that their felt interests are not their real interests (Lukes, pp. 23f.).

Similarly, in his *Lectures on Ideology and Utopia*, Ricoeur points out that a chief function of ideology is to legitimate authority and thus oil the wheels of the authoritarian machine. 'No system of leadership, even the most brutal, rules only by force, by domination. Every system of leadership summons not only our physical submission, but also our consent and co-operation' (Ricoeur, p. 13). We ought then to be aware of the power of the social structure to influence the kind of people we are. Reich suggests that 'every social order produces in the masses of its members the structure which it needs to achieve its main aims' (Reich, p. 57; cf. p. 66). If this seems unnecessarily mythological in its personification of society, it remains true that, as Fromm points out, the dynamics of social life cause people to want to do what they have to do for the well-being of society (1982, p. 62). There is then a concealed, tacit and largely unrecognized exercise of authority; discussions of the explicit exercise of authority need to be conducted against this background.

This insight informs Peter Miller's distinction between domination and power. While domination acts upon individuals or groups 'directly counter to their aspirations or demands', power acts on the subjectivity of the individual, influencing their objectives and aspirations. It operates deviously by promoting a distorted subjectivity (Miller, p. 2).

(e) The choice of terms inevitably involves some semantic arbitrariness. Thus Leonardo Boff defines domination as authority without consent (Boff, p. 40), which aligns him with Miller, while Stephen Sykes claims that authority without consent is tyranny (Jeffery (ed.), p. 22). This is to take power as a subdivision of authority, instead of vice versa, as appears to be the convention.

Shütz defines authority as 'the interpretation of power'. It differs from force in having to give an account of itself acceptable to those who obey it (Shütz, p. 14). But, as we shall see, authority was not always answerable to its subjects.

Weber's terminology is controversial, but he appears to use *Macht* to stand for domination—the ability to carry out one's will despite resistance—and *Herrschaft* for authority in the specific sense of 'imperative control'—'the probability that a command with a given specific content will be obeyed by a given group' (Weber, p. 152).

Talcott Parsons's definition assimilates power to authority, but throws in sanctions to boot. It is couched in his characteristic rebarbative style:

Power then is generalized capacity to secure the performance of binding obligations by units in a system of collective organization when the objects are legitimized with reference to their bearing on collective goals and where in case of recalcitrance there is a presumption of enforcement by negative situational sanctions. (Ng, p. 70)

(f) The Jungian thinker Hans Dieckmann has distinguished three types or modes of authority: first, authority as compulsion or force; second, authority as reputation or prestige; and third, authority as competence or expertise (Dieckmann, p. 23). This concise taxonomy may be regarded as a sliding scale in which the assimilation of authority to power steadily diminishes.

In authority as compulsion, authority is swallowed up in power as coercion. The correlation with the use of punitive sanctions renders authority extremely vulnerable. No one has *carte blanche* to perpetrate violence on another with no questions asked. Even police, prison warders or troops, who do indeed have the authority to use force, are liable to discipline if they misuse it. It is a measure of how much our ideas of authority have changed in the modern world that authority shines out the more clearly the further it becomes detached from force.

In authority as reputation or prestige, in which I would include authority by consent and delegated authority, the power aspect is muted but not absent. The bearskinned sentries at Buckingham Palace are symbols of glory rather than coercive power. The absence of battledress suggests that they do not expect to use the modern weapons that they nevertheless carry. But by their presence they remind us that the sovereign is titular head of the armed forces. There are no soldiers outside 10 Downing Street, only policemen.

In authority as acknowledged competence or expertise, in which knowledge and wisdom are given their due, the element of power is almost entirely absent—though the possibility remains, as with every human relationship, of the abuse of authority by manipulation or intimidation. Even in authority as competence, the survival requirement is present. An expert numismatician has an extremely limited sphere in which his or her authority is recognized, simply because human survival or happiness does not depend a great deal on the study of ancient coins. An expert transplant surgeon commands authority in a wider sphere because he or she has power over life and death.

Where do the clergy stand on this spectrum? Their authority lacks prestige—except for archbishops, cardinals and popes—and rests entirely on competence. They are the experts with knowledge of divine mysteries, and with the tools of their trade —wise speech, prayers, sacraments—they can put individuals in touch with a transcendent source of well-being, of healing of the personality, of salvation. (It is worth anticipating here a point that will emerge strongly at a later stage—that the more the authority of the clergy is assimilated to competence, the higher the standard of training and of theological, liturgical and inter-personal skills that will be expected of them.) In a profound sense, the clergy too have the power of life and death, but unless there is general recognition that what the Church's ministers have to offer is of supreme value, of ultimate concern, that authority resting on spiritual competence will gradually atrophy. In a society seemingly oblivious of God, how many will sell all they have to obtain the pearl of great price?

The three forms of authority—coercion, reputation and competence—may be found together in varying proportions. An American president may have enormous power, but a questionable reputation and less wisdom than his awesome responsibilities require. A pope has a worthy personal reputation and a degree of numinosity that belongs to his office and on which he can trade, but may deprive himself of vital information or criticism. An Indian guru has wisdom, if not knowledge, and a resulting reputation and prestige in some quarters, but is almost entirely lacking in the power to compel individuals and enforce his will (cf. Dieckmann, p. 230).

These reflections bear out Dieckmann's comment that 'we have to understand authority, not as a static, unchanging innate principle, granted to man by the will of God, but as a principle capable of changing, of taking different forms of growth and development towards certain goals which are, in the final analysis, determined by our value systems' (p. 233). Although authority is 'a principle which is inherent in nature, which is connected with the instinctual force of structure and order, and which can be observed even on the level of animal life' (p. 234), it takes different forms in response to human needs—economic, social and spiritual. Authority cannot be absolutized or reified: it is always based on a relationship and never exists as a mere object like a mountain, which is always there even if no one is around (p. 231). But that relationship may be either oppressive or liberating. There is a relationship between master and slave that is oppressive and inhibiting, and there is a relationship between a teacher and pupil that is liberating and enabling (cf. Fromm, 1942, p. 141).

What conclusion can we draw from this survey? To add yet another definition may seem unhelpful! Yet we certainly need a working formula to give coherence to our discussion. It would seem to command broad support if we defined *power* as *the capacity to obtain compliance with one's will*, and *authority* as a form of power where *compliance is willingly given* because it is accepted that that will has the right to be complied with. Here we come up against the central paradox of authority: the fact that obedience to legitimate authority is regarded as voluntary and is based on consent rather than coercion, yet at the same time is felt to be mandatory or obligatory, in contrast to persuasion which can be legitimately resisted (cf. Wrong, p. 50).

It is this paradox that is at the centre of contemporary ferment regarding authority in the Church. What are the grounds on which that authority is to be regarded as mandatory or obligatory? How have those grounds shifted over the centuries, particularly since the Enlightenment and the emergence of our modern pluralistic situation? To what extent can those grounds be re-established? Is it desirable for this to be done? What form of authority will emerge at the end of this process and will it be recognizably the same authority that the Christian Church has traditionally claimed to exercise over the faith and morals of the faithful?

3

Authority and Enlightenment

LEAR: What wouldest thou?
KENT: Service.
LEAR: Whom wouldest thou serve?
KENT: You.
LEAR: Dost thou know me fellow?
KENT: No, sir; but you have that in your countenance which
      I would fain call master.
LEAR: What's that?
KENT: Authority.

Shakespeare, *King Lear*, I, iv, 24ff.

'Authority', wrote Hannah Arendt, 'has vanished from the modern world.' Both in practice and in theory, she insists, 'we are no longer in a position to know what authority really is' (Arendt, pp. 91f.). Does Arendt mean, then, that whenever we discuss authority, we are talking about something that no longer exists? Indeed she does. In the present chapter, I want to discuss the proposition that authority has suffered a profound deconstruction at the hands of modernity. This is a necessary preliminary to asking how authority can be reconstructed in a liberating, therapeutic form to meet the demands of our 'post-modern' situation.

When Arendt asserts that authority has vanished from the modern world, she presumably means by 'the modern world' the world that rose out of the ashes of the fascist totalitarian régimes that had cast a shadow of death over her own life as a member of the European

Jewish intelligentsia and had provided the spur to some of her most influential writings. It is true that the authority of the state, with its hierarchical and quasi-hieratic leadership of fascist demagogues enveloped in a halo of numinosity, that could once call for the unquestioning sacrifice of the nation's manhood in wars of conquest, is discredited. As we see vividly in Eastern Europe today, people will fight and, if necessary, die for their cause, but that cause, though it may be a nationalistic one, is populist and democratic and frequently alienated from government, even revolutionary government. Only among fundamentalist movements—Islamic and sectarian Christian—and within the Roman Catholic Church's official self-perception does full-blooded authority still reign. Elsewhere it has indeed vanished from the modern world.

To appreciate Arendt's point we must discern the essential features of traditional authority. Though always legitimated (see below, Chapters 5 and 6), authority is *sui generis*. It demands and receives unqualified obedience because of what it is. It is self-authenticating. It has no need to appeal either to reason or to sanctions.

First, naked authority should be distinguished from reasoned *persuasion*. As Hobbes put it: 'Command is where a man says *do this* or *do not this* without expecting other reason than the will of him that says it' (Wrong, p. 35). Authority does not depend on agreement being attained on the basis of reason. 'Where arguments are used, authority is left in abeyance', says Arendt (Arendt, p. 93). David Watt has pointed out that 'a person who understands a pronouncement completely, with all the reasons for it, can no longer accept it on authority' (Watt, p. 106). It is not authority's role to act as midwife to rational understanding. As Bacon said, 'Authority may compel belief, but cannot enlighten understanding'. Authority does not need to stoop to persuade. 'In so far as we attempt to persuade or to bargain, we approach one another as equals, whereas authoritative relationships exist between unequals' (Watt, p. 27). The order of persuasion is egalitarian—it involves a meeting of minds on an equal basis—but the order of authority is hierarchical—its deliverances are promulgated *de haut en bas*.

Secondly, authority should be distinguished from *coercion*. It does not depend on sanctions to enforce it. As Arendt argues, 'Where force is used, authority itself has failed' (Arendt, p. 93). Force may ensure compliance but it does not earn respect. But there are, of course, other—more subtle—ways of obtaining compliance that fall

27

short of physical coercion: threats of unpleasant consequences, withdrawal of privileges, ostracization. These may be equally effective where the threats are believed or the privileges valued, but rather than reinforcing the authority of those powers that operate them, they surely undermine it. They unmask such purported authority to be in reality merely naked power.

While Hannah Arendt welcomed the demise of authority in the modern world, Kierkegaard deplored it. In *The Book on Adler*, translated as *On Authority and Revelation*, Kierkegaard sets up the supreme paradigm of authority as *apostolicity*. Apostolicity is correlative to *divine* authority and belongs to the sphere of the transcendent. Authority is thus irreducible. We do not enhance the authority of the apostle Paul by praising the sublimity of his style! Genius has nothing to do with authority. 'I am not obliged to obey Paul because he is clever . . . but I must submit to Paul because he has divine authority' (Kierkegaard, p. 107). To ask whether the king is a genius before we obey him is *lèse-majesté*. To honour one's father merely because he is a distinguished man is impiety. Authority emanates from a transcendent source. What makes true authority 'qualitatively decisive' is its origin and source. All we need to know is, who is speaking. When Jesus Christ speaks of eternal life and the local curate speaks of eternal life, they are both saying the same thing; 'both statements, aesthetically appraised, are equally good. And yet there is an eternal qualitative difference!' (pp. 113f.).

What, then, is authority, asks Kierkegaard: 'Is authority the profundity of the doctrine, its superiority, its cleverness? Not at all. . . .' Authority lies not in the content but in its source. '*Authority is the specific quality which comes from another place*' (p. 110).

While authority belongs to the sphere of transcendence, in the sphere of immanence, as Kierkegaard puts it, that is, at the purely human level, man to man *qua* man, '*authority cannot be thought, or it can be thought only as vanishing*' (p. 111). Thus while for Arendt authority has already vanished, for Kierkegaard, it is constantly vanishing from the modern world—insubstantial, fleeting, unable to maintain itself.

Taking our bearings from Kierkegaard, we need to set the demise of authority in a longer historical perspective. Arendt was writing in the shadow of the destruction of terroristic totalitarian régimes, but Kierkegaard was prophesying the spiritual bankruptcy of modernity in the liberal-bourgeois society of Western Europe in the mid-nineteenth century. Kierkegaard's world was that created by the

Enlightenment and its ensuing corrective, the romantic aesthetic.

The Enlightenment mounted a conscious, concerted challenge to the unquestioned authority of the *ancien régime* in Church and state. The divine right of kings and the divine right of the Church were its twin targets. The Pope crowned the Emperor and the Emperor defended the Pope. Pius IX was battening down the hatches of the Vatican against the harsh winds of Enlightenment when he refused to 'reconcile himself with, and accommodate himself to progress, liberalism and modern civilization'. His successor Leo XIII was still insisting at the end of the century that 'the highest duty is to respect authority' (*Libertas Praestantissimum*, 1888) and that 'to despise legitimate authority, no matter in whom it is invested, is unlawful; it is a rebellion against God's will' (*Immortale Dei*, 1885).

For the classical thinkers of the Enlightenment, appeal to authority was the antithesis of reliance on one's own reason. From Descartes to Kant authority was held responsible for the binding and gagging of human reason. As Gadamer has pointed out, the distinction between authority and individual reason is in itself a legitimate one. If unquestioning submission to the prestige of authority excludes one's own judgement, then authority becomes tyrannical. But this option does not rule out the possibility of authority being a vehicle of truth—to be recognized by one's own discernment. As Gadamer claims, within the Enlightenment the very concept of authority became deformed and was taken as demanding blind obedience. This is the notion of authority that, as Arendt insists, has vanished from the modern world. But the death of the unreconstructed oppressive authority of the *ancien régime* makes it possible for a liberating concept of authority to come to light—an authority that is based, as Gadamer puts it, not on the subjection and abdication of reason but on the acknowledgement of a superior knowledge, insight and judgement (Gadamer, pp. 246ff.).

The Enlightenment attempted to transfer the seat of authority from dogma to reason, from tradition to experience and from society to the individual. Kant defined Enlightenment as the coming of age of mankind, its emergence from a state of self-imposed immaturity and deference to the guidance of another in matters of intellect, not because he is intellectually superior but simply through lack of confidence, courage and decision (Kant, pp. 54–9). Here Kant was articulating the logic of the Protestant Reformation. As Fromm has put it: 'The development of modern thinking from Protestantism to

29

Kant's philosophy, can be characterised as the substitution of internalised authority for an external one' (1942, p. 143). This, of course, is to alter radically the whole nature of authority. There is indeed an authority, but it is the authority of freedom, of self-determination, of the imperative quest for truth. Isaiah Berlin has eloquently captured the Enlightenment spirit of autonomy:

> I wish my life and decisions to depend on myself, not on external forces of whatever kind. I wish to be the instrument of my own, not of other men's acts of will. I wish to be a subject, not an object; to be moved by reasons, by conscious purposes, which are my own, not by causes which affect me, as it were, from outside. I wish to be somebody, not nobody; a doer—deciding, not being decided for, self-directed and not acted upon by external nature or by other men as if I were a thing, or an animal, or a slave incapable of playing a human role, that is, of conceiving goals and policies of my own and realising them. . . . I wish, above all, to be conscious of myself as a thinking, willing, active being, bearing responsibility for my choices and able to explain them by references to my own ideas and purposes. I feel free to the degree that I believe this to be true, and enslaved to the degree that I am made to realise that it is not. (Berlin, p. 131)

Unless we reckon with this inalienable claim of the human spirit, we cannot understand the great movements of emancipation that have shaped modern history and culture—from the emancipation of oppressed classes in the great political revolutions, to the emancipation of races in the civil rights movements, to the emancipation of women in the feminist movement that is now confronted in the Church with the remnants of ideologically motivated opposition to the acceptance of women as autonomous individuals and equal partners.

Mention of women's freedom brings with it the question of patriarchy. Patriarchy is the historical norm of human society. It stands for order, hierarchy, authority, formal relationships, rigid responses —all undergirded and sustained by the repression of spontaneity, of liberty, of libido. Without subscribing to all of Freud's theories of sexual energy and Reich's extreme and obsessive development of them, it is nevertheless apparent that *social authoritarian patriarchy* is the model and basis of *intellectual authoritarian ideology*. Both Freud's picture of the rebellion of the sons of the tribal chief in the primal horde, who had monopolized the women, and Reich's description of the patriarchs 'depriving the women, children and adolescents of their sexual freedom, making a commodity of sex and placing sexual interests in the service of economic subjugation', illustrate the connection between sexual repression, patriarchal authority and economic interests. Neither need we accept Reich's myth of primal matriarchy in order to appreciate the contrast between patriarchal authority and matriarchal spontaneity: 'In terms of patriarchal demands, the innocent sensuousness of matriarchy appears as the lascivious unchaining of dark powers' (Reich, p. 122). As Reich points out, economic dependence is not enough to preserve the authoritarian family. Sexual repression, especially of the wife, though also of the children, is demanded too:

> For the suppressed classes, this dependency is endurable only on condition that the consciousness of being a sexual being is suspended as completely as possible in women and in children. The wife must not figure as a sexual being, but solely as a child bearer. Essentially, the idealisation and deification of motherhood, which are so flagrantly at variance with the brutality with which the mothers of the toiling masses are actually treated, serve as means of preventing women from gaining a sexual consciousness, of preventing the imposed sexual repression from breaking through and of preventing sexual anxiety and sexual-guilt feelings from losing their hold. (p. 138)

One suspects that the opponents of women's emancipation in the Church, who are also indisputably the upholders of patriarchal authority, tradition, hierarchy, formalism in ritual, doctrinal purity, and so on, understand full well that the two causes stand or fall together. The question for Christian theology is whether the biblical image of the Fatherhood of God entails necessarily the traditional notions of hierarchy, authority and submission that arguably belong not to an unchanging ontological reality, but to specific and contingent stages of human society—stages that are now being superseded.

For it has been argued by the critical theorists of the Frankfurt School—notably Horkheimer and Marcuse—that the economic determinants of patriarchy, with its concomitants of the suppression of sexuality, external, heteronomous authority playing upon guilt-feelings and a strong super-ego, no longer obtain. In 'The End of Reason' (1941), Horkheimer claimed that psychoanalysis had 'triumphed over the moral law through its discovery and unmasking of

the father in the super-ego'. Freud's aetiology of conscience, obligation and guilt-feelings as the instruments of sexual repression and
patriarchal authority had subverted patriarchalism psychologically
just when the traditional bourgeois family structure was being
subverted economically anyway. Freud's theory was (to borrow
Hegel's phrase) 'the owl of Minerva' which 'took its flight when the
shades of dark were already gathering over the whole sphere of
private life'. With education largely out of the hands of the family
and the child's future livelihood no longer bound up with that of his
father, the bourgeois authoritarian family has become economically
obsolete. Just as the child 'sees through' his father, so the individual
'sees through' society with its claims and sanctions. 'The father may
still possess a super-ego, but the child has long unmasked it',
Horkheimer concludes. The relation of father and son is now free
to become that between comrades, the older and more experienced guiding and supporting the novice. Horkheimer goes as far
as to pronounce that, since Freud, the relation between father
and son has been reversed: 'The child, not the father, stands for
reality' (1941, pp. 376f., 381; cf. Horkheimer and Adorno (eds),
pp. 139ff.).

In his 'Study on Authority' (1936), Marcuse showed that the head
of the family (*pater familias*) was endowed with almost priestly
consecration in Protestant theology to fill the vacuum of paternal
authority created by the abolition of the Roman Catholic hierarchy
and priesthood (Marcuse, 1973, pp. 74f.).

Luther's concept of *Beruf* (calling, vocation) raised parenthood to
the level previously accorded to the religious life. In his exposition of
the Fourth Commandment (our Fifth Commandment) in the Large
Catechism, Luther states that honouring one's parents is 'the
greatest work that we can do, next to the sublime worship of
God. . . . For God has exalted this estate of parents above all others;
indeed he has appointed it to be his representative on earth.'
Moreover, 'out of the authority of parents all other authority is
derived and developed. . . . Thus all who are called masters stand in
the place of parents and derive from them their power and authority
to govern'; a ruler is the father of all his people (Luther, pp. 382ff.).

In his exposition of the Commandment, Calvin too insists that
parents are owed 'reverence, obedience and gratitude' and that 'the
submission yielded to them should be a step in our ascent to the
Supreme Parent'. The principle is of the broadest application, for
we should recognize in all who are placed in authority over us the

hand of providential government to whom God communicates his own authority (*Institutes*, II, viii, 35–8: Calvin, vol. II, pp. 344ff.).

Marcuse went on to expose this apotheosis of parenthood, and of fatherhood in particular, as later providing a convenient legitimation of oppressive capitalist economic structures. Marx, he pointed out, 'confronts authority as a relationship of dependence in the capitalist process of production' (1973, p. 131) and distinguishes 'the ideological appearance of the bourgeois family from its material reality' in which the women and children were exploited (pp. 141f.). What was claimed as 'eternal' and 'natural' in family relationships was merely the reflex of economic constraints. The concept of the family was 'an indifferent abstraction' open to distortion and exploitation (ibid.).

The twin functions of authority and obedience have traditionally rested on the fact of a split in human nature, between mind and body, conscience and instinct, society and nature. This state of estrangement or alienation is the *sine qua non*, the indispensable condition, of authoritarianism. Marcuse in particular has questioned whether in our 'one-dimensional society' this condition any longer obtains. In the administered society, in which physical needs are satisfied and the mental world is conditioned by the ubiquitous media of communication, the individual becomes one with his environment. 'Its productivity and efficiency, its capacity to increase and spread comforts, to turn waste into needs, and destruction into construction, the extent to which this civilisation transforms the object world into an extension of man's mind and body makes the very notion of alienation questionable' (1964, p. 9). Society exercises control by satisfying the needs it has first created, with the result that 'people recognise themselves in their commodities' (ibid.). The 'triumph and end of introjection' is reached when 'people cannot reject the system of domination without rejecting themselves, their own repressive instinctual needs and values' (1969, p. 26). Marcuse also points out that this actually represents a deeper regression into alienation, one so serious that the possibility of liberating oneself from it becomes questionable indeed, as 'the self-propelling conservative continuum of needs' proceeds with unchecked momentum (1969, p. 27).

Marcuse therefore suggests that the term 'introjection' is no longer appropriate to the way in which the individual assimilates and makes his own the expectations and assumptions of his society, for 'introjection implies the existence of an inner dimension distinguished from and even antagonistic to the external exigencies—an

33

individual consciousness and an individual unconscious *apart from* public opinion and behaviour. The idea of "inner freedom" here has its reality: it designates the private space in which man may become and remain "himself".' Today, however, this private space and inner integrity has been eroded by the conditions of mass culture and mass production, resulting in an 'immediate identification' of the individual with his society (1964, p. 10). In this process of 'the pacification of existence' the voice of the super-ego has been stilled, authority is manipulative and concealed. This is the nemesis of Enlightenment with a vengeance: the progress of liberty has culminated in a state of collective passive acquiescence. The social determination of consciousness is all but complete. Under these circumstances, how can a radical change in consciousness, as the first step in changing social existence, ever come about?

Marcuse's gloomy conclusion is that 'such a revolution is not on the agenda'. But the combination of economic crisis and 'radical enlightenenment' could generate at least a 'pre-revolutionary situation' (1969, pp. 61f.). In recent years we have witnessed in Eastern Europe precisely such a combination, in which economic catastrophe has provided the occasion for the emergence of radical reforming programmes. Some Christian churches exhibit a state of 'collective passive acquiescence' in a totally administered situation where sacramental 'commodities' are the reward for obedience. What will it take to subvert this collusion between authority and the faithful? What combination of 'radical enlightenment' theologically and economic crisis will undermine inflexible centralized structures?

The socio-genetic evolution of the human race has been characterized by what Waddington called 'authority-acceptance'. Survival demanded group cohesion and that could only be achieved by accepting authority. The converse of this, of course, is that authority can only operate within a defined group identity. 'Identity and authority are mutually implicative', assert Robertson and Holzner (p. 5). 'Authority and identity grow up together', states Swanson (Robertson and Holzner (eds), p. 191), 'and pervasive difficulties in one simply pervasive problems in the other.' He continues:

> Authority is legitimate power. Identity is a sense of personal continuity, of personal resources, of engrossing purposes, of one's being authorized to follow where these purposes may

lead. It is also the faith that the course of one's life is meaningful.

Therefore:

> There is no authority except in the context of identity: power is not legitimate unless people find it meaningful and good: unless it is the source of their own empowerment, a resource for their pursuit of their own purposes and a conserver of a social order within which they can act today and can anticipate acting in the days ahead.

Similarly:

> Identity is impossible without authority. Without authority there is no source of personal empowerment and no stable, meaningful order within which purposes can be pursued and a coherent life career formulated.

Where society is fragmented by the assertion of local identity, whether on a community, regional or national basis, as characterizes our late twentieth-century world, identity is devolved to the smaller unit and authority becomes dispersed. But a fragmented, localized, almost private source for authority sustains no authority at all in Arendt's full-blooded sense. It has become so qualified as to be almost unrecognizable. If it is to survive—and the needs of a society's identity demand that it must—it will have to emerge as a very different animal.

Arendt writes:

> Authority, resting on a foundation in the past as its unshaken cornerstone, gave the world the permanence and durability which human beings need precisely because they are mortals— the most unstable and futile beings we know of. Its loss is tantamount to the loss of the groundwork of the world, which indeed since then has begun to shift, to change and transform itself with ever-increasing rapidity from one shape into another, as though we were living and struggling with a Protean universe where everything at any moment can become almost anything else. (Arendt, p. 95)

The undermining of absolute, self-sufficient, reified religious authority in the West (the Islamic Near and Middle East is a different matter), authority we accept unquestioningly for what it is, and not because we fear the consequences of disobedience or happen to agree with its demands, is one of the most important factors for a critical ecclesiology to take into account. The Church no longer has the power to enforce its will: threats of divine retribution hereafter would not be taken seriously—it is not assumed that the Almighty will underwrite all that the Church insists on in his name. That leaves reasoned persuasion, discussion and argument, but the outcome of that process cannot be predicted. The Church must curtail its requirements and wait upon the emergence of consensus in those areas where a common mind is still required.

The demise of real authority is a situation that will increasingly have to be taken into account, willy nilly. But my aim in the discussion that follows is to show, by reference to the philosophy of science and critical theory, that the inevitable is actually the desirable, indeed the only acceptable basis for a reconstructed theory of 'authority' in the Church, modelled on our experience of mutual acceptance, reasoned agreement where possible, tolerance of disagreement where necessary in other areas of human interaction—marriage and the family, teaching, pastoral care and the therapeutic situation.

4

The Thirst for Authority

As the taboo on introducing the subject of religion into polite dinner-table conversation suggests, everyone knows that we tend to be at our most subjective, irrational and dogmatic in this particular area of life. Why is this? To find an answer, we need to look at what is known about the psychological dynamics of authority relationships and relate it to the process of identity formation in the individual.

AUTHORITY AND IDENTITY

We are all engaged in the lifelong process of seeking or making our identity. Identity has to do with who we are, how others see us, what we are worth, and where we fit in. Identity formation takes place through the twin psychological mechanisms of projection and introjection: we project our incipient and inchoate ideals and images of selfhood on to the external screen, as it were, of another person who enjoys stronger identity, more prestige and greater authority (a parent, leader or superior), and then reappropriate those ideals and images by introjection. Through identification with a putatively superior other, our own sense of identity is enhanced (cf. Avis, 1989a, ch. 1).

But there are various permutations of this process. The seeker after self-identity—and that includes all of us at various stages of life and to varying degrees—can adopt one or more of three courses of action. I give them in descending order of psychological worth.

First, we may seek an interactive confrontation with our projected ideal figure through a process of feedback in depth to a self that retains its own integrity throughout. This would be a beneficial encounter, therapeutic in appropriate circumstances and leading to a wholesome strengthening of identity and a deeper integration of the personality. At the highest level, something very much like this is surely meant by the practice of 'the imitation of Christ', in which prayer and contemplation lead to more Christlike action.

Second, we may engage in projection without introjection, attempting to change our personality by modelling ourselves on a leader or hero figure in a crude imitation of external traits—that is to say, without true interaction or deep engagement. The result would be a superficial, ephemeral and unsatisfying deviation in identity— an identity without integrity. In the Oxford of the 1830s, undergraduates aped Newman's physical mannerisms in walking or preaching, but none of Newman's genius rubbed off on them by their so doing. Today's teenagers copy the clothes and hairstyles of their pop idols. In our consumer society, as Luckmann points out, an individual can easily pick up 'a pre-fabricated identity, advertised, marketed and guaranteed by the identity-producing agencies', the mass media (Luckmann, p. 116).

The third, even more worthless, possible means of identity enhancement is to make a desperate attempt to fill the void of identity with worthless gimmicks, cheap thrills, by saturating the consciousness through compulsive sex, speed, drugs, deafening music or even soppy romantic novels.

Sow a thought: reap an action. Sow an action: reap a habit. Sow a habit: reap a character. Sow a character: reap a destiny. A personality pattern, once established, is reflected in the whole of one's life. The individual's psychological make-up, with all its limitations and distortions, serves as a grid through which the whole of his or her world is perceived and encountered. Where these distortions are severe or the make-up is pathological, the repercussions on society can be traumatic, the areas of politics and religion being the most vulnerable.

The classical exercise of research into this area of social psychology was carried out by T. W. Adorno and others in the later 1940s, during Adorno's exile in the United States, into the roots of anti-Semitism and the making of the fascist mentality, and published under the title *The Authoritarian Personality* in 1950. After nearly a thousand pages of data and interpretation, the authors came to the following conclusion:

38

The most crucial result of the present study, as it seems to the authors, is the demonstration of close correspondence in the type of approach and outlook a subject is likely to have in a great variety of areas, ranging from the most intimate features of family and sex adjustment through relationships to other people in general, to religion and to social and political philosophy. (Adorno *et al*., p. 971)

The authors went on to delineate two personality types, not as absolutes, but as models to represent two syndromes at the opposite poles of personality formation: the *repressive* and the *spontaneous* personalities.

THE AUTHORITARIAN PERSONALITY

The repressive or authoritarian type is one whose life is marked by domination—his own experiences of domination and repression in childhood forming a psychological burden that he transfers to his own children and imposes on his whole world.

The characteristics of this type are brilliantly portrayed by M. Brewster Smith in a collection of studies published in 1967 which reviewed the thesis of *The Authoritarian Personality* in the light of subsequent research. The typical candidate for the sobriquet 'authoritarian personality' is 'the basically weak and dependent person who has sacrificed his capacity for genuine experience of self and others so as to maintain a precarious sense of order and safety that is psychologically necessary for him'. Such a person is alienated from himself and therefore from others:

The authoritarian confronts with a facade of spurious strength a world in which rigidly stereotyped categories are substituted for the affectionate and individualised experience of which he is incapable. Such a person is estranged from inner values and lacks self-awareness. His judgements are governed by a primitive conventional moralism, reflecting external standards towards which he remains insecure since he has failed to make them really his own.

His dualistic world betrays overcompensated psychological insecurity:

In his world, the good, the powerful and the ingroup merge to stand in fundamental opposition to the immoral, the weak,

the outgroup. . . . His underlying feelings of weakness and
self-contempt commit him to a constant and embittered
struggle to prove to himself that he really belongs to the strong
and good, and that his ego-alien impulses, which he represses,
belong to the weak and bad. (Kirscht and Dillehay (eds),
pp. vif.)

The authoritarian stereotype (for that is what it is—a stereotype;
not every case that broadly fits the description is walking around
with the whole gamut of hang-ups!) is characterized by middle-class
conventionalism and rigidity, uncritical submission to authority and
acceptance of rationally inexplicable beliefs and superstitions, emotional immaturity, and lack of imaginative sympathy and 'tender-
mindedness'. On the other hand, he is aggressive and condemna-
tory towards those who violate his values and beliefs, destructive and
cynical towards all that is most 'human' in culture and society, and
intolerant of uninhibited sexual behaviour since he is alienated from
his own sexuality (Kirscht and Dillehay (eds), pp. 5f.). He perceives
radicalism—political, religious or ethical—as an affront: for it challenges 'the whole system of resistances which are binding down the
illicit impulses of the personality'. Deviation is disloyalty, sacrilege
or immorality, depending on the context. In the obsessive thinker,
the dogmatist, writes Lasswell, 'the conscience may be four years
old' and like an 'introjected nursemaid' construes all change as disobedience (1951, pp. 175ff.). He is a 'closed-minded' person who
lacks the ability to deal with new ideas or facts that do not fit his
cognitive outlook. He has what Festinger calls a low 'tolerance for
dissonance': he cannot abide cognitive inconsistency or ambiguous
situations (Festinger, pp. 266f.; cf. Merton, pp. 8ff.). He seeks
prematurely to resolve unfamiliar situations and falls back on the
clearly defined belief system and package of values that is under-
written by his chosen external authority. His dogmatism is a defensive reaction against doubt—a doubt of which he is unaware
(Lasswell, 1951, p. 175). However, as Adorno *et al.* make abun-
dantly clear, all this repression and striving against reality is building
up trouble for the future, and a breakthrough of the repressed weakness, fear and dependence is to be expected when a crisis is reached
that is just too much for the individual's defences.

The authoritarian personality inhabits a split world. He tends
to go in for the 'dichotomous dramatization of roles'—parent/
child, man/woman, us/them, pronounced 'ingroup–outgroup

cleavages'—based on radical stereotyping. Thus, Adorno *et al.* conclude, 'a basically hierarchical, authoritarian, exploitative parent–child relationship is apt to carry over into a power-orientated, exploitatively dependent attitude towards one's sex-partner and one's God'. The dominant type fears weakness, clings to what is strong, and projects this on to his chosen leaders and his God. His psychological make-up contains the ingredients of the fascist mentality (Adorno *et al.*, p. 971).

The scheme deployed by Adorno *et al.* has not gone unchallenged. It is clearly one-sided. As David Watt put it: 'By their oversimplified dichotomizing, intolerance of ambiguity, and undue preference for symmetry, the authors have left room only for the one variety of authoritarians they were looking for, the xenophobes (particularly the antisemites) and all but obscured others, notably communists' (Watt, pp. 20f.). Here Watt accuses the researchers of the very vices that they identified in their subjects—conceptual rigidity, dualistic thinking and intolerance! However, while Watt's *tu quoque!* may relativize their conclusions, it certainly does not invalidate them.

AUTHORITY AND MODERNITY

In *The Fear of Freedom*, written during the Nazi ascendancy, Erich Fromm traced the conditions conducive to the emergence of the authoritarian personality in the evolution of the modern world. Through the Reformation and the rise of capitalism, human beings became progressively more autonomous, self-reliant and critical, but at the same time more isolated, anxious and afraid. In religion, 'Protestantism made the individual face God alone' (Fromm, 1942, p. 94). In society, the individual became subordinated to the economic system, an insignificant cog in the machine. At the same time as he has been given his freedom, through his religion and through the provision of the means of subsistence, modern man has been devalued and rendered insignificant. The burden of creating his own value and significance existentially is unbearable: he looks for a means of escape from his dilemma. Dostoyevsky wrote in *The Brothers Karamazov* that 'man has no more agonising anxiety than to find someone to whom he can hand over with all speed the gift of freedom with which the unhappy creature is born' (I, p. 298). Freedom is the tragic destiny of modern humanity for it is inseparable from

41

alienation. Fromm, the Jewish socialist intellectual who had left Germany in 1932, observes with sad cynicism that millions of his fellow countrymen were as eager to surrender their freedom as their forefathers were to fight for it (1942, p. 2).

Fromm's thesis is the one later researched by Adorno *et al.*: that the authoritarian character 'represents the personality structure which is the human basis of Fascism'. Nazi ideology, Fromm asserts, appealed especially to the lower middle class, those who had been squeezed between the theoretically available religious and political liberty on the one hand, and the grinding pressures of the capitalist system on the other. Nazism appealed to their love of what is strong and successful and their loathing of weakness and failure; their pettiness, hostility to what is different; the asceticism and puritanism of their work ethic; their narrow-mindedness, suspicion and envy; and their thriftiness—both emotional and pecuniary (1942, pp. 141, 182f.).

It is a disturbing paradox of modern history that, parallel to the advance of so-called Enlightenment and autonomy in the modern world, there has emerged wave after wave of irrational authoritarianism and repression. That irrational authoritarianism has undoubtedly been called forth, not only by socio-economic factors in our 'late capitalist' society, but also by powerful psychological needs in the unconscious of modern humanity. Horkheimer observed that 'the whole political, religious and philosophical literature of the modern period is filled with praise of authority, obedience, self-sacrifice and the hard fulfilment of duty' (1972, p. 90). Mannheim has drawn attention to the way in which a highly complex society deprives the mass of its members of any grasp of how it functions and where it is going:

> The fact that in a functionally rationalised society the thinking out of a complex series of actions is confined to a few organisers . . . has led to the growing distance between the élite and the masses and to the 'appeal to the leader'. . . . The average person surrenders part of his own cultural individuality with every new act of integration into a functionally rationalised complex of activities. (Mannheim, pp. 58f.)

However, though socio-economic factors create the conditions for the cult of the leader, the actual mechanism involved is psychological.

COLLECTIVE CONSCIOUSNESS

Freud attempted to give a psychoanalytical explanation for the phenomenon of mass identity described by Le Bon. The individual caught up in a mass movement abdicates the critical, moral faculty of the ego-ideal and succumbs to his unconscious. Like the aborigine, the infant and the neurotic, he is swayed by instinctive needs and weak in discriminatory power. He thinks by association and by means of images rather than concepts, flies to extremes and exhibits a harsh intolerance. He is submissive to authority, wanting to be ruled and even oppressed, rigidly conservative in his views and, untroubled by contradictions, he feeds greedily upon illusions. In Le Bon's phrase, he has a 'thirst for obedience'. Freud explained these traits in term of his libidinal theory. The removal of social and moral inhibitions in mass consciousness gives libidinal pleasure to the individual. The group or mass is constituted by libidinal or love ties to the leader and one's fellows. Freud suggests that in its extreme form, in which the group becomes fused together and mobilized for action as a 'horde', its members have surrendered their ego-ideal and adopted a common object in its place. That common object is the identity of the group, symbolized by its leader (Freud, pp. 104ff., 124f., 147).

As this account implies, the authoritarian leader can be seen from one point of view as merely a function of the collective unconscious. He has the ability to perceive intuitively and articulate the unconscious longings of the mass. He promises them what they deeply crave. There is an isomorphism of psychological structure between the individual and his leader. As Adorno puts it: 'The leader can guess the psychological wants of those susceptible to his propaganda because he resembles them psychologically and is distinguished from them by a capacity to express without inhibitions what is latent in them' (Arato and Gebhardt (eds), p. 132). Such leaders (and Adorno undoubtedly has fascist demagogues in mind) are oral character types, with a compulsion to speak incessantly. Their uninhibited but largely associative speech presupposes, he suggests, a temporary relaxation of ego control. Though cunningly aware of the dynamics involved in manipulating the collective unconscious, the leaders nevertheless become to some extent the tools of the powers they have catalysed and unleashed. Though Freud rejected the theory of collective hypnosis as an explanation for 'mass hysteria', Adorno speaks metaphorically of the 'collectivisation of the hypnotic spell' (in Arato and Gebhardt (eds), pp. 132, 137).

It is significant to Adorno as well as to Freud that the phenomenon of group identity is displayed in the army and the Church. As conservative and hierarchical bodies, they are fertile soil for the development of collective consciousness, group thinking and the diminution of critical response. This prompts the reflection that if the Church were less hierarchical, it would become less conservative, more flexible and more securely grounded in reality rather than illusion. Autonomy and spontaneity are not the most conspicuous attributes of the mainstream Christian churches and it may well be that in this respect they share the fate of our Western industrialized mass culture. Adorno suggests that the secret of fascist propaganda is that 'it simply takes men for what they are: the true children of today's standardised mass culture, largely robbed of autonomy and spontaneity' (Adorno *et al.*, p. 134).

Psycho-social research suggests that authoritarianism emerges when instinctive libidinous impulses are repressed through economic necessity aided and abetted by ideological constraints. Repression takes its revenge as dammed-up psychic energy surges back in the form of aggression. The nature of this aggression is sado-masochistic. It is directed against itself and against its world. It punishes itself and it punishes others. Social structure and ideological guilt-mongering work hand in hand in this process. As Horkheimer suggests:

> For the foundation of the authority-orientated character it is especially decisive that the children should learn, under pressure from the father, not to trace every failure back to its social causes but to remain at the level of the individual and to hypostatize the failure in religious terms as sin or in naturalistic terms as deficient natural endowment. The bad conscience that is developed in the family absorbs more energies than can be counted, which might otherwise be directed against the social circumstances that play a role in the individual's failure. The outcome of such paternal education is men who without ado seek the fault in themselves. (1972, p. 109)

Horkheimer finds the correlative of this notion of authority sustained by guilt in Protestant theology. Here, he suggests, authority is not conceived of as a personal engagement between two unequal parties, but rather as 'an inalienable property of the superior being, a qualitative difference'. And that is to reify authority, to abstract it

44

from its seat in personal values and existential development. 'It is not because God is wise and good that men owe him reverence and obedience', according to Protestant theology, but because he is God, is supreme (1972, p. 103). To extrapolate, we could say that it is not because the Church is the Body of Christ, the Christian family of love and solidarity, that we owe it our allegiance, but because it is the Church with a claim to reified authority! Similarly, it is not because the Pope is wise and good and is in a position to consult the whole Church that Catholics owe him obedience, but because he is Pope and claims the legitimation of the God who is God and the Church that is the Church. So too, it is not because the Bible is the earliest witness to the event of Jesus Christ and our only source of his words and deeds that it is to be heeded, but because it is the Bible, is absolute and has the legitimation of the God who is God, the Church that is the Church and the Pope who is Pope!

SADO-MASOCHISM?

One means of escaping the pressures of modern society is to surrender to authority. But the person who craves authority also loves to wield it. As Russell puts it: 'The power impulse has two forms: explicit, in leaders; implicit, in their followers' (B. Russell, p. 15). The authoritarian personality is thus a sado-masochistic type. For the later Freud, sado-masochism was the product of the combination of the death or destruction instinct with the sexual drive, *Thanatos* with *Eros*. The essence of sadism is 'pleasure in the complete domination over another person' (Fromm, 1942, p. 135). But this lust for power is rooted, psychologically, in weakness; that is to say, in the reverse of sadism—masochism (p. 139). For Fromm, sado-masochism is not necessarily neurotic: it may merely denote an extreme character type, the authoritarian character. For the sado-masochistic person is characterized by his attitude towards authority. 'He admires authority and tends to submit to it, but at the same time he wants to be an authority himself and have others submit to him' (pp. 140f.). In Dieckmann's Jungian perspective, the sado-masochistic compulsion to rule and to be ruled belongs to the psychic structure, not only of those who possess authority and enjoy wielding it, but also of those who protest against it. 'These rebels for freedom change into oppressive and compulsive dictators the very moment they succeed, and are compelled to become rulers because their own psychic structure forces them to do so' (Dieckmann, p. 240).

The sado-masochistic nature of authoritarianism is suggested by Adorno's remark that 'the leader image gratifies the follower's twofold wish to submit to authority and to be the authority himself' (Adorno *et al.*, p. 127). He is at once the master and the slave: slave to his own master but master to his own slaves. The provenance of the sado-masochistic personality in repressed and perverted sexuality is surely not controversial, though I would certainly not want to exclude structures of social repression that might be seen as analogous to the sexual repression of the individual. Wilhelm Reich claimed in *The Mass Psychology of Fascism* that the architects of Nazi strategy knew that 'sadism originates from ungratified orgastic yearnings' (p. 224), and exploited their potential ruthlessly. (I am not here concerned with Reich's linked assertion that religious experience—'mysticism'—is also the product of repressed and frustrated 'orgastic yearnings': that contention needs to be considered in the context of a study of eros and the sacred: cf. Avis, 1989b, pp. 121ff.) The essential point here is that Reich saw the totalitarian, authoritarian potential of mass production and mass culture, in both its capitalist and its collectivist forms. Fascism, he insisted, is 'only the organised political expression of the average man's character'. It is universal in the Western world. 'Fascism is the basic emotional attitude of the suppressed man of our authoritarian machine civilisation.' In its express manifestations, fascism is 'the sum total of all the irrational reactions of the average human character'. All of us carry the 'elements of fascist feeling and thinking' in our psychic structure (Reich, pp. 15f.).

Reich's perception that, because sadism is but the obverse of masochism, masochistic religion contains the potential for 'flipping over' into a sadistic crusade, is important. Authoritarianism presides over both masochistic religions of suffering and sadistic religions of persecution. Fascism 'transposes religion from the "otherworldliness" of the philosophy of suffering to the "this worldliness" of sadistic murder' (Reich, p. 17). Richard Holloway has made the same connection: with the Nazi holocaust in mind, Holloway is acutely aware that the Christian religion, considered as a constellation of human projections and constructions, has a lot to answer for. A culture based on 'fear, guilt and the radical interiorisation of a sense of profound failure' produces 'a truly horrifying civilisation'. 'Centuries of guilt and dread stoked the boilers of the

Holocaust. . . . The "Final Solution" is the realised eschatology of the doctrine of hell.' Holloway points to the moral:

> The penal view of the universe, the perception of it as a great testing ground for eternity, seems to rebound upon it, visiting its children with the very penalties they sought to avoid, building into them a guilt they cannot assuage, a sense of demand they cannot appease and a fatal longing for order that can only be satisfied by the exaction of a terrible price. (Holloway, pp. 76ff.)

In her study *Oppression and Liberty*, Simone Weil attempted to capture the essence of the spirit of obedient servitude:

> It seems to those who obey that some mysterious inferiority has predestined them to obey for all eternity, and every mark of scorn—even the tiniest—which they suffer at the hands of their superiors or their equals, every order they receive, and especially every act of submission they themselves perform confirms them in this feeling. (Weil, p. 145)

It is the sado-masochistic exchange at the heart of authoritarianism that makes it not merely tiresome and unfortunate but morally unacceptable. It certainly justifies W. K. Clifford's dictum: 'There is one thing in the world more wicked than the desire to command—and that is the will to obey' (cited, Y. Simon, p. 148).

'The will to obey'—if the sado-masochistic interpretation of the thirst for obedience seems somewhat melodramatic, a more humdrum interpretation is suggested by Stanley Milgram and his notorious series of experiments where a cross-section of individuals were persuaded to administer what they believed were electric shocks of steadily increasing intensity and danger to an unfortunate guinea-pig who provided the appropriate screams and contortions. Though some agonized as they stepped up the supposed voltage, their deference to the authority of men in white coats, who impassively requested their compliance in the name of science, overcame conscience and judgement. Milgram concluded that 'the essence of obedience consists in the fact that a person comes to view himself as the instrument for carrying out another person's wishes, and he therefore no longer regards himself as responsible for his actions' (Milgram, p. xii). This disappearance of a sense of responsibility was the most far-reaching consequence of submission to authority (p. 8). Milgram's ultimate observation was that 'a substantial portion of people do what they are told to do, irrespective of the content of the act and without limitations of conscience, so long as they perceive that the command comes from a legitimate authority' (p. 189).

This is a more disturbing interpretation than the sado-masochistic reading of the Freudians because it brings the possibility of destructive and vicious acts, in obedience to self-proclaimed authority, within the scope of many, if not most, ordinary people. It also raises the question of whether, by its continual exaltation of authority and inculcation of obedience, the Church is not a prime accomplice to this nightmare.

OPEN OR CLOSED?

In his classic study *The Open and Closed Mind*, Milton Rokeach offers a complementary perspective on the psychological causes of dogmatism and authoritarianism. Rokeach's thesis is that our attitudes, values and commitments are determined by 'pre-ideological' or 'primitive' beliefs. These have the status of unquestioned assumptions, it being a condition of a primitive belief that it is assumed that virtually everyone shares it. Predominant among these 'primitive' beliefs are our perception of our own identity and of the social world we inhabit. Is the world basically friendly or unfriendly? Are people in general to be trusted or feared? Is the future to be regarded with a sense of security or a sense of apprehension? (Rokeach, pp. 40ff.) Rokeach suggests that these (stereotyped) perceptions, which give rise to the (stereotyped) open or closed mind, derive from experiences in infancy: they may be 'a function of the breadth or narrowness of identification with others', which, in turn, may depend on 'the extent to which ambivalent feelings towards parents are permitted within the family atmosphere'. Where feelings of, say, rivalry, resentment, independence or jealousy are not allowed to be acknowledged and expressed, they become repressed into the unconscious, so generating (clinical) anxiety (p. 361).

However, Rokeach is clear that he does not regared the defensive, dogmatic personality as neurotic: the closed mind is merely a stereotype of 'normal' behaviour. 'Primitive' beliefs that the world is hostile are not pathological, though there are 'primitive' beliefs which are irrational and pathological, such as that represented in claustrophobia, because no external evidence or authority can disconfirm them. And there are extreme cases where the closed mind is 'nothing more than the total network of psychoanalytic defence mechanisms organized together to form a cognitive system and designed to shield a vulnerable mind' (pp. 42, 70).

Rokeach defines a person's belief system as open or closed to the extent that he can 'receive, evaluate and act on relevant information . . . on its own intrinsic merits, unencumbered by irrelevant factors in the situation' arising either from oneself ('unrelated habits, beliefs and perceptual cues, irrational ego-motives, power needs, the need for self-aggrandizement, the need to allay anxiety', etc.) or from outside oneself ('the pressures of reward and punishment arising from external authority', etc.). An individual's open belief system is signalled by its resistance to external reinforcement, the promise of reward or the threat of punishment. A closed belief system, conversely, is revealed by its inability to distinguish the validity of information from the evaluation of its source as either friendly or unfriendly, authorized or unauthorized (pp. 57f.). In a closed system the power of an authority is correlative to the sanctions—rewards and punishments—it can administer (p. 62). A closed system is the product of an external threat. This applies equally to individuals, who are 'disposed to accept or to form closed systems of thinking and believing in proportion to the degree to which they are made to feel alone, isolated and helpless', and to societies—and here Rokeach takes the history of the Roman Catholic Church as an example—that can be shown to become defensive, absolutist, paranoid and coercive as the external threat to their belief system intensifies (pp. 69, 376–88).

There is no belief system without a disbelief system: by accepting certain views, we automatically exclude others. The human drive to know and to understand the world is moderated by the drive 'to ward off threatening aspects of reality'. It is salutary to remind ourselves that all belief systems serve these two powerful and conflicting sets of motives at the same time. The ideal, if we would know the truth and yet retain a coherent 'system', is (Rokeach suggests) to be open as far as is possible and closed as far as is necessary (pp. 67f.). Significant for us also is Rokeach's reflection that the alternative to accepting or rejecting others on grounds of the congruity of their beliefs with ours is to accept them unconditionally, as parents accept their child and spouses love one another. He adds that this is the ideal of religions such as Christianity that teach the 'brotherhood of man' and love of the neighbour as oneself, as it is also of the whole approach of psychotherapy that speaks of symptoms not of sins

49

(p. 63) and is grounded in a relation of unconditional mutual acceptance between therapist and client.

Rokeach's open-minded person corresponds to the 'spontaneous personality' of Adorno *et al.*, which is characterized by affectionate, accepting, inter-personal relationships on the basis of mutual equality. He or she is more secure and, as a result, more flexible, adapting to the different requirements of different kinds of relationship and reaping greater satisfaction from them (Adorno *et al.*, p. 971). This is Lasswell's 'democratic character' with his openness to others, capacity for friendship, shared multiple values (he does not obsessively have all his eggs in one basket), and confidence in the human potential for good (derived from the satisfaction of infant needs by the mother). Freed from irrational anxiety, his energy is available for positive social ends (Lasswell, 1951, pp. 482ff.). Such persons have no compulsion to project dreams of domination or Walter Mitty delusions of grandeur on to a leader figure, a Führer, with whom they identify and who has the power to turn their fantasies into actuality. Nor do they need to project a divine father-figure of interventionist omnipotence who will vindicate them against (imagined) enemies, see that they are all right, and ensure that they are rewarded for their rectitude.

FUNDAMENTALISM AND THE THIRST FOR AUTHORITY

The typology surveyed in this chapter suggests that in some of us there is a need, a longing, for authority and that this represents a psychological weakness that it would not ordinarily be right to indulge. One might well want to ask whether there is evidence of the domination syndrome in the leadership of the Christian churches; of the 'dichotomous dramatization of roles' between say, clergy and laity, men and women, leaders and led; of the paranoid projection of occult dark forces on to those who hold a different theological position and venture to raise critical voices against the teaching authority of the Church, reposing as it claims upon the impregnable rock of holy tradition, the papal office or inerrant holy scripture. In reactionary conservatism, whether Protestant or Roman Catholic, we find the same techniques familiar from fascist propaganda: stereotyping, clichés and unceasing repetition, which serve to 'sharpen the modes of reaction, endow the platitudes with a kind of self-

The Thirst for Authority

evidence, and disengage the resistance of the critical consciousness' (Horkheimer and Adorno (eds), p. 172, cf. pp. 196–81: 'Prejudice').

How does Protestant fundamentalism fit into this picture? In a study of leadership and authority in the Christian Church it is not part of our brief to venture into the controversial interpretation of Islamic or Jewish fundamentalism (see Caplan (ed.); Gill, ch. 2). However, two identifying features of the fundamentalist phenomenon are relevant here (Gill, p. 22).

The first feature is cognitive: fundamentalism is marked by its commitment to scriptural absolutism. In the case of Protestant fundamentalism, the Bible constitutes 'the supreme tangible sacred reality' (Barr, p. 36). The absolute authority of the Bible is the primary tenet of Protestant fundamentalism and as such serves as a major strengthener of group identity. The Bible—both formally, as a symbol or shibboleth, and materially, in its fundamentalist interpretation—is also the principal ideological weapon of fundamentalism in its crusade against error. But this brings us to the second aspect.

The second feature is sociological: fundamentalism stands for a counter-cultural ideology—an ideology that stands over against the modern, Western, pluralistic, liberal civilization. While, as Gill points out, 'there is no single counter-cultural opposition to modernity apparent within fundamentalism' (Gill, p. 33), every form of fundamentalism is counter-cultural in its own way—adversarial, polemical and dualistic.

Militant Islam, for example, works with a dualism of light and darkness, heavenly forces and devilish powers that is worthy of the Book of Revelation. No doubt that is why Salman Rushdie's *The Satanic Verses* cut so deeply into the Islamic consciousness—it reversed the dualistic moral ontology of militant Islam, the equivalent of 'the unforgivable sin' in the Gospels.

Protestant fundamentalism is equally dualistic and adversarial. In its case, the evil emissaries are the liberal theologians of the decadent mainstream churches (Barr, p. 101). This dualism entails exclusivism whereby all members of those churches who are not card-carrying fundamentalists are deemed not to be true Christians (Barr, pp. 310, 338). They need to submit to the truth of the fundamentalist gospel of the inerrant authority of the Bible, substitutionary atonement and a literal eschatology. They still need to be saved. As Barr has pointed out, in fundamentalism, all relations with non-conservative theology are purely polemical (p. 163). He perceptively suggests

51

that fundamentalist dualism is not an understandable response to the minority status of fundamentalist groups but a manifestation of paranoia (my word, not his—but as someone with extensive personal experience of fundamentalism and conservative evangelicalism, I am not dependent on Barr's analysis for these judgements). Barr suggests that, for fundamentalists, 'liberalism' and 'modernism' are 'no more than necessary myths, bogeys that have to be held up for execration and ritual contempt on every possible occasion' (p. 104)—on a level, one might suggest, with the chanting, portrait-waving and effigy-burning of fanatical crowds in the Middle East. This conclusion is endorsed, in less emotive language, by Caplan in a recent comparative survey: 'The character and contours of fundamentalism can best be drawn by reference to some notional and significant ''other''. This opposition may delineate and represent for the participants themselves a substantive arena of religious beliefs and practices, thus enabling them to establish definitive boundaries' (Caplan (ed.), p. 21).

The cult of the leader or father-figure, the frisson of submission to authority, the craving for absolutes and the thrill of belonging to an army that can never be defeated are all factors to be reckoned with in any discussion of the nature of authority in the Church and of the commitment of the individual Christian. While the appeal to authoritarian political movements, making a total claim on the allegiance of their members, has been subjected to ideological analysis, notably by the thinkers of the Frankfurt school, building on the work of Freud (himself dependent on Le Bon and McDougall), and the same has been done by others for fringe religious sects, we do not see much preparedness on the part of the churches to take a critical and informed look at the nature of their own power and influence over the lives of individuals. It would indeed be a breakthrough if the churches themselves were to sponsor a professionally conducted enquiry into the tensions of freedom and restraint, autonomy and authority, individuality and solidarity, factors that create the conditions for growth in spiritual maturity. This chapter has simply attempted to set out some of the conceptual tools relevant to such an enquiry.

5

Sacred Status and the Bureaucratic Church

TRADITION, BUREAUCRACY AND CHARISMA IN ACTION

On a grey November morning in London, Westminster Abbey—that historic national shrine which is under the jurisdiction of the Crown—is filled with processing archbishops, bishops, deans, archdeacons and clergy in their impressive convocation robes, and with lay representatives of the dioceses. The newly elected General Synod of the Church of England is being inaugurated. The Queen is present as the supreme governor of the Church of England and (though a lay person) she is the first to receive holy communion from the archbishops of Canterbury and York. The Lord Chancellor (the highest law officer of the land) and the Foreign Secretary are present. The sermon is preached by a scholar who has been dean of a cathedral and Regius Professor of Divinity in both the most ancient universities of the land. The Roman Catholic cardinal archbishop of Westminster and leaders of other Christian traditions are present, though not all receive communion at this Anglican altar. After the service, the dignitaries and the rank and file of the new synod proceed to Church House, Westminster, in the shadow of Parliament, to receive the blessing and encouragement of Her Majesty the Queen. Status reigns supreme. Traditional authority is in the ascendant. Sacred offices are filled by sacred persons clothed with sacred insignia.

The formalities over, the synod quickly becomes aware that it is there to deliberate and to legislate. Members remember that they have been elected on a controversial ticket and by a highly complex system of voting. The Secretary General sits on the chairperson's right to advise about the conduct of business. He represents the considerable and complicated bureaucratic machine that services the Church of England's system of government. The registrar sits on the left of the chair to advise on legal and constitutional technicalities. Reports, statistics, accounts, lists and notices are pumped out at a steady rate. The First Church Estates Commissioner is at hand to remind the synod at frequent intervals that it must count the cost before deciding anything. Any major decisions will be referred to diocesan and even deanery synods and, if the required support is forthcoming, return for a two-thirds majority in which bishops, clergy and laity will vote separately. Process is all. Bureaucracy is in control. Rational–legal authority dominates the Christian conscience convened in council.

The matter is open for debate. Bishops, clergy and laity queue to speak. Who will sway the mind of the synod? The view of the elected standing committee carries the most sway—its role is to listen to opinion and to obtain all the necessary information. The two archbishops are next in influence: is it by virtue of their office or due to their personal stature and ability and their representative role, close to the heart of the Church? Ideological considerations and loyalty to partisan party groups figure third in influence on the synod. But the diocesan bishops, who stand for sacred status more than any other order, have the least influence. 'The diocesan bishop's voice was the one which, in synod, had the least claim to attention' in deciding individuals' voting intentions (Medhurst and Moyser, pp. 212ff., 218). Except, that is, when an impassioned plea is made to the synod's conscience and heart, as on one famous occasion when the Bishop of Durham, David Jenkins, made an emotional apologia. Charisma briefly flares. The synod is set alight. Outstanding gifts and personalities can sway the synod. It will respond to charisma, even if calmer counsels will ultimately prevail when 'emotion is recollected in tranquillity'. But true charisma is at a premium in any Anglican conclave—and I suspect in a Roman Catholic conclave or that of any other historic Christian Church that has been compelled to adapt its structure and conduct to the modern world. Why is this? To answer that question, we need to look more closely at the concepts of status, role and charisma, using Max Weber's celebrated threefold analysis of authority.

ROLE AND STATUS

As a member of a particular community or organization, I have a particular *role*. This role gives me a certain *status* and my status enhances my role. Any authority that I may exercise is a function of my role and status. If I am a bishop, for example, I have a role in the pastoral care and teaching ministry of the Church that extends beyond my immediate diocesan responsibilities. With that role goes a certain status both in the Church and in the wider society. In the Church a bishop is leader, teacher and ruler. In the wider society he is a pillar of the establishment. My role and my status carry a certain authority—moral, spiritual and legal authority within the Church; moral authority only beyond it.

Role is not identical with status or with actual behaviour: it is 'the sociological context of individual behaviour' (Jaques, p. 25). Role is something given by society with which the individual is invited to collude. It involves what Charles Handy calls a 'psychological contract'—an unspoken understanding between the individual and the community. 'What one asks of people, how one controls people, how one organises people, how one rewards people, all depend on the psychological contract' (1985, pp. 47f.).

Status is what legitimates a role. It consists of the rights and obligations that enable a role to be performed. You cannot have a role without a status or a status without a role. Role is the dynamic aspect of status and status the static aspect of role. Role activities are carried out from status positions. While role is a basically neutral term, status is a loaded term. As Dorothy Emmet points out, people do not usually mind changing their role, but they are afraid of losing their status (1972, pp. 26ff.). Several aspects of role-function are worth bringing out.

(a) ROLES ARE HUMAN CREATIONS
You can have a God-given status, particularly, as we shall see, in a traditional society, but we do not so readily speak of a God-given role. Roles are manufactured to serve the purposes of the society. We cast people in a particular role by placing certain expectations on them. When we withdraw those expectations, the role disappears. For example, under the influence of the feminist movement, the Church has revised upwards its expectations of what women can contribute to the public life of the Church; it is prepared to give women a role in ministry. But to do this it must tackle the more contentious

issue of what status this would give women, for with status goes authority: status carries overtones of the sacred in a traditional society.

(b) ROLES RELATE TO PERSONALITY

Although our roles are cast by society, rather like parts cast for a play, a role that begins as a mask or persona may soon become absorbed into the personality. As we practise our role it shapes us inwardly. This is to be expected, for roles are not handed out entirely arbitrarily, but awarded to those who are regarded as suitable. There has to be a modicum of role-receptivity for a role to 'take'. Those accustomed to give orders in their work role find it difficult not to be peremptory when they return home. Furthermore, roles fulfil personality needs—for esteem, responsibility, human relationships. While some have a need to rule, others have a need to obey—though it does not follow that either should be gratified without stringent safeguards.

(c) ROLES PRODUCE PROBLEMS

It is seldom that a role is a perfect fit. It has been suggested that conflict between the role and the personality is 'a function of discrepancies between the pattern of expectations attaching to a given role and the pattern of need-dispositions characteristic of the incumbent of the role'—in other words, between instrumental needs and individual requirements (Getzels in Bennis *et al.* (eds), p. 383). One manifestation of this conflict between an imposed role and the personality struggling to fulfil it is the phenomenon of 'role confusion'. Jaques has suggested that role confusion is 'an unconsciously motivated defence' against the anxiety generated by the disjunction between personality and role (cited Sofer, p. 213).

A person may suffer from 'role overload' when the expectations placed upon him may be too great (even though the actual workload may be tolerable). As Jaques has commented, one of the signs of a too low capacity for a role is that the incumbent of the role will tend to seek more and more information 'hoping that somehow a solution will come floating out through the facts. It never does' (Jaques, p. 301).

At the other extreme, one may be the victim of 'role underload', where the organization's expectations are not commensurate with a person's ability. This has little to do with actual workload, but rather with the extent to which the exercise of discretion is called for within it. In the Church we are becoming accustomed to the notion of clergy stress through overwork, but stress through lack of sufficiently challenging work also needs recognition and remedy. Jaques describes the frustration of the 'under-stressed': 'He is being deprived of that vital freedom to test his capacity at full stretch; that is to say, he is being deprived of the opportunity to maintain his relationship with reality over as wide a spectrum as possible. Part of his world will be missing' (Jaques, p. 286). Gradations, matched by differentials (to be discussed in the last chapter of this book), are vital in a calling such as that of the parochial clergy, where much of the work is routine.

Both these situations will tend to be destructively stressful. Rather than working a person hard in a suitable role—a form of pressure that is beneficial and productive, like making a diesel engine pull hard—they put an intolerable strain upon a person precisely because the role is unsuitable. Handy distinguishes between beneficial 'role pressure' and harmful 'role strain' (1985, p. 65).

Roles also generate problems when an individual is the recipient of several different and conflicting roles. 'Role conflicts occur whenever a role incumbent is required to conform simultaneously to a number of expectations which are mutually exclusive, contradictory or inconsistent' (Getzels in Bennis *et al.* (eds)). This is particularly the dilemma of the leader who has to combine a supportive, unifying role with a prophetic, challenging role, reconciling with rebuking, maintenance with mission.

Max Weber's classical analysis of types of authority, set out in his *The Theory of Social and Economic Organization*, is an indispensable tool for understanding the varying relations between role and status. Talcott Parsons described Weber's typology of authority as constituting 'the most highly developed and broadly applicable conceptual scheme in any comparable field' (though this judgement is now more than forty years old; see Weber, p. 77). Weber's analysis sheds light on the traditional authority-character of the Church and on present trends that are undermining that authority-structure.

According to Weber (d. 1920), every 'corporate group' (*Verband*) is defined by acknowledged boundaries and an internal differentiation of roles in which authority is distributed. Each has its chief (*Leiter*), administrative staff (*Verwaltungsstab*) and members (Weber, pp. 145f.). A corporate group may belong to one of three authority types: the 'traditional', the 'rational–legal' or the 'charismatic'. Here we shall consider the first two, reserving the third for the next chapter.

TRADITIONAL AUTHORITY: SACRED STATUS

Clearly the Church belongs to the *traditional* category. This, according to Weber, rests on 'an established belief in the sanctity of immemorial traditions and the legitimacy of the status of those exercising authority under them' (Weber, p. 328). In the traditional scheme it is believed that the rules of the community—its beliefs and practices—have always been the same. Any innovations will be presented as restorations. The leader issues decrees to which obedience is due, but the 'administrative staff' apply pressure to the chief to restrict his power.

The Church is the paradigm of traditional authority (*Herrschaft*—imperative control). It believes that it perpetuates the primitive Christian community and that its leaders stand in a succession that goes back to the apostles. It does not admit innovation. If there is Reformation, it must be to restore the face of the ancient catholic Church. If women are to be admitted to its priesthood, it must be shown that the Founder entrusted women with a significant ministry, even if he did not include them among his chosen apostles. If doctrinal or ethical problems arise, the binding solution will be found in the trust deeds of the Church, the holy scriptures or the ancient undisputed traditions. Archbishops and bishops bear the rule, but they are hedged about by synods and staffs. Even the Pope is curtailed by the Curia.

The Church is, in Weber's terms, a typical 'hierocratic' group because its clergy enjoy a monopoly in the dispensation of spiritual privileges and sanctions:

> An imperatively co-ordinated corporate group will be called a 'hierocratic' group if . . . it employs 'psychic' coercion through the distribution or denial of religious benefits ('hierocratic coercion'). A compulsory [i.e. one is born into it] hierocratic association with continuous organization will be called a 'church' if and in so far as its administrative staff claims a monopoly of the legitimate use of hierocratic coercion. (Weber, p. 154)

But a group, where membership was solely by conversion and not by birth, where there was no clear division between clergy and laity and consequently no monopoly of authority by the clergy, would be a *sect* (p. 156).

Status rather than role is the key to traditional authority within the Church. In traditional ecclesiology, which we still find at its most explicit in the Roman Catholic Church, status is first *hierarchical*: it is maintained that the concept of hierarchy is written into the trust deeds of the Church, from the Lord's commission to Peter onwards, in such a way that for the Church to cease to be hierarchical would be for the Church to cease to be the Church. Secondly, this hierarchical understanding of status is *essential*: it is the channel through which sacramental grace is mediated to the Church for the salvation of souls. If the hierarchy fails, God's saving purpose fails. Thirdly, the indispensable salvific hierarchy is *sacred*: it is not merely the channel of the sacred but is sacred itself. It is untouchable. It is not a candidate for reform or coercion. As Joseph de Maistre put it: 'It does not belong to man to change institutions for the better. . . . Hence the automatic aversion of all good men for innovations. The word reform . . . will always be suspect to wisdom' (cited Lasswell, 1949, p. 60).

As we have seen in previous chapters, the institutional churches are no longer living in the Middle Ages, with its hierarchical, feudal structure of society. They have survived somehow, at the cost of enormous trauma, into the modern world where claims to status and unquestioned authority are highly suspect and where every component of our complex and competitive society must be able to justify its existence and pay its way. Any claim to status is highly vulnerable in this environment and no one owes it a living. Even the Royal Family has to earn its keep. Traditional authority is on the defensive. Though the trappings of office may remain, the justification of office has subtly changed its ground from status to role.

Role, but not status, is acceptable, provided that it is a role sanctioned by the prevailing canons of society—and that means the utilitarian criteria of productivity and efficiency. Even the papacy, which Macaulay envisaged serenely surviving the ruins of civilization in the third millennium, no longer simply projects itself as the embodiment of God-given absolute authority (*plenitudo potestatis*) —though none of those historic claims has in practice been retracted or even moderated—but is increasingly seen as a focus of unity and the enabler of communion. In other words, the papacy now has a role. In the modern world, authority is acceptable to the extent that it does a useful job and does it well. Competence is the criterion.

BUREAUCRATIC AUTHORITY

Weber's second type of authority structure is the *rational-legal*. This is the authority of an impersonal order and operates by applying a set of rules from which there is no appeal. It depends on the efficient functioning of a bureaucracy (Weber, pp. 328ff.), so I propose to call this type *bureaucratic authority*. Roles, defined by rules, are the key to bureaucratic authority.

Just as traditional authority reflects the static, sacral conception of the cosmos and society of the early Middle Ages, so too the bureaucratic type reflects the diversification and complexification of role—both of individuals and of organizations—in an industrial society. Bureaucracy marries the pluralism of society to the sophistication of technology. This can be seen to be true of the Church also where centralized bureaucracy attempts to impose cohesion on a pluralistic movement—a cohesion that is facilitated by modern methods of communication. This cohesion is a necessary condition of the Church's functioning effectively within itself and presenting itself to other organized aspects of the pluralistic, technological society outside its boundaries—relating to other organizations and communities.

In his important work *Bureaucracy and Church Reform*, Kenneth A. Thompson has traced the progressive bureaucratization of the Church against the background of the differentiation of institutional spheres in the developing pluralistic society in nineteenth-century England:

> The organizational response of the Church of England to social change has been viewed as part of a process of differentiation of institutional domains within the social structure, in which the Church, like other institutions, gained increasing autonomy and had to develop its separate administrative and governmental organization. At the same time, that organization had to be capable of relating itself to other differentiated institutions, and so it adopted many of the common operational criteria of formal rationality. (Thompson, p. 212)

This process generated a tension between developing more auto-nomous governing agencies, informed by bureaucratic rationality, on the one hand, and maintaining identity 'as a coalition of diverse principles of authority and doctrine' that had given the Church of England its character as a comprehensive national religious estab-lishment, on the other (p. 214). Taken to excess, the pursuit of instrumental efficiency, by maximizing formal, bureaucratic ratio-nality, fails to take account of the distinctive character and the ultimate goals and values of the Church (p. 238). Centralized bureaucratic Church government distorts the pattern of dispersed and self-balancing authority in a broad Church.

Bureaucratic authority does not impinge significantly on the laity. They are all volunteers; the Church has no bureaucratic hold over them. It can only exercise moral authority and persuasion. The laity constitute the precarious power-base of the Church as an institution. This Church cannot afford to alienate them. It must constantly woo the laity, indulge their predilections as far as possible, sooth their susceptibilities. Since lay people pay the piper, inevitably they will ultimately call the tune.

But bureaucratic authority certainly constrains the clergy—I speak of the Church of England, but I suspect that our experience is symptomatic of wider trends. The Anglican clergy enjoying a free-hold living have largely been their own masters (the sexism of that expression is intentional!). They have understood their role and have been confident that the means of livelihood would be provided to enable them to fulfil it. Until recently, they were in no sense the paid servants of the laity, their stipends being provided entirely out of historic endowments. They were entrusted by their bishop—whether by design or neglect—to get on with the parochial task. As a calling, they were not doing the job for the money or any incidental benefits ('perks'). It might be said that the Church's administrative staff were there to enable the clergy to follow their vocation without undue anxiety about the necessities of life.

All that has begun to change and the clergy are being transferred from a *vocational* to a *contractual* relationship to the Church. While ecclesiastical patronage and 'the parson's freehold' still moderate the trend to bureaucracy, the number of freehold livings has been drastically reduced by pastoral reorganization. Most new appoint-ments are fixed-term contracts to serve in team ministries. And at the time of writing, there are moves afoot to make virtually all ecclesiastical offices leasehold. More than half of the clerical stipend is paid by the laity through direct giving: this makes the clergy accountable and underlines the importance of scrupulous and meticulous book-keeping. Clergy are reluctant to spend time filling in forms—they accept that this is inevitable when it is intended to convey essential information, but tend to resent it when it constitutes a form of monitoring, supervision and 'checking up on' them. The administrative structure of the Church of England—from the Church Commissioners to the diocesan staff—now tends to appear more in the light of an employer rather than of an enabler.

The growing practice of ministerial assessment can confirm this impression if it is felt that 'they' are assessing 'us', rather than the whole Church, from bishops and archdeacons down, engaging in a process of mutual and reciprocal assessment and encouragement. In a recent study of appraisal, Michael Jacobs comments: 'I take it as axiomatic that where there is an appraisal system in operation, bishops and their staffs should be appraised as well' (Jacobs, p. 56). Jacobs notes the dilemma inherent in an appraiser trying to handle authority and care at the same time (p. 66). Noting that appraisal has little effect on improving performance and that it may prove deleterious, Handy advocates separating the roles of judge and counsellor (1985, pp. 260ff.; cf. Argyris, p. 261). The negative overtones of the current (salutary) moves towards making the clergy more accountable could be avoided if, as Handy suggests, formal appraisal schemes were reformulated as 'self-development contracts', because ' "appraisal" sounds like judgement, not help, looking backwards not forwards, smacking of authority not partnership' (1989, p. 184). It would appear to follow that 'appraisal' should be taken out of the hands of diocesan officials, who are seldom trained and qualified to handle this delicate operation constructively, and put into the hands of those who are—mainly lay people together with clergy without canonical responsibility for the subject of the appraisal. Such ministerial development programmes would be totally confidential and the legitimate personnel-management needs of the diocese would be met by an interview with the bishop, say every three years.

A quasi-contractual relationship between the clergy and the Church as an institution no doubt brings a number of benefits. It keeps the clergy on their toes to know that they are being monitored. It encourages them to be more efficient in keeping accurate records of the numerous, but mostly very small, financial transactions that pass through their hands, and not to imagine that spiritual-mindedness is an excuse for financial mismanagement. The leasehold contract for clergy in teams makes it easier to deploy human resources where they are needed and to solve human conflicts—at least superficially—by moving clergy away from a source of friction.

But it also carries a number of penalties. Firstly, and obviously, it entails an increase in the number of paid administrative officials—and then the question arises whether the increase in received income through greater efficiency is not cancelled out by the expansion of paid bureaucracy.

Secondly, it can contribute to demoralization among the clergy. They do not have an easy time in their parishes. They are the mediators in numerous conflicts and the recipients of both positive and negative projections (and those that are positive, and see the minister as an ideal figure—saint, father-figure, husband-substitute, or whatever—can be more dangerous than projections that are negative and which transfer experiences of bad parental or marital relationships on to the clergy). Clergy need to be affirmed and encouraged. Where contractual status replaces vocational status, this is often experienced as demeaning because it discounts the primary motivation of the ordained ministry. It takes the clergy at face value—as the paid employees of the Church—not at the value they thought they had in the eyes of God and the Church when the bishop laid hands upon them and entrusted them with their cure of souls.

Thirdly, the trend towards a contractual status for the clergy creates a division between them and the administrative machine. If they sense that they are not trusted to pursue their calling with integrity without supervision, they will tend to reciprocate that distrust. There will be a sense of 'What are they trying to put over on us now?' Where rules are enforced, those on the receiving end will tend to 'work to rule'. It will be more difficult to sustain the sense that 'we are all on the same side' and must pull together as a team. It becomes unconvincing to attempt to trade on the idea of the diocese (for example) as a family. Where requirements are insisted on, individuals may do less than they did voluntarily before and will sometimes do it with a bad grace. Where status is affected, individuals will want to come together for mutual support and form professional associations (a trade union for the clergy?) to negotiate pay and conditions of service. The price of 'rational–legal' authority is the risk of alienation.

Fourthly, the trend towards a contractual relationship between the clergy and the Church's bureaucracy creates a dichotomy between the way that the clergy relate to their parishes, and the way that they relate to the diocese. In the parish, the clergy are dealing almost without exception with volunteers who are giving their time, energy and money of their own free will—people who have to be won over, persuaded and encouraged, led but not driven, to do what they do. The *modus vivendi* between the clergy and the Church's administrative structure should follow the same pattern as far as possible. Co-operation freely given, working together towards agreed goals, a sense of sharing in a common fellowship, should mark the relations between Church leaders and the parochial clergy. Canonical obedience to one's bishop does not contradict this, but instead reinforces it. Because it is canonical obedience within the terms of one's commission, it binds the priest to his or her vocation. Managerial directives, on the contrary, ignore vocation and bypass canonical obedience. They thus set up a disturbing tension between the way a priest operates and responds in relation to the parish, and the way he or she operates and responds in relation to the administrative structure. This dichotomy can only be an impediment to the mission of the Church, sapping the dedication of the clergy and undermining their position in the parish.

ROLE AND RULE

Under bureaucratic authority, roles are defined by rules—not by traditional status. Geoffrey Vickers has noted that the transition from status to contract that marked the emergence of the modern world was in fact 'the transition from a state in which positions, with their accompanying roles and status, were traditionally defined and filled by largely traditional means, to one where they could be freely defined and redesigned and their occupants freely appointed and dismissed' (1973, p. 29). Though this has made possible the development of huge institutions, complex enough to meet the economic demands of the modern world, it has left us with the legacy of how to resolve the conflicts that it generates.

As Vickers has pointed out, 'conflicts are best resolved where the parties share strongly . . . the constraints and assurances of membership' (1973, p. 141). United in a common cause, all members of an institution can devote their energies to dealing with conflicts *ab extra*. But once the assumption gains credence that the cause, the well-being, of one component of an organization (say, the workers or the parochial clergy) is not identical with the cause of another component (say, the management or the Church's administrative structures), then energies are turned inward and conflict is focused on the internal dynamics of the organization. Productivity (say, manufacturing, or the mission of the Church) suffers as a result. All conflicts affect the relations of the parties concerned 'by weakening or strengthening the constraints and assurances which they feel as implicit in their common membership'. So the management of conflict requires to be even more closely concerned with preserving those relationships within the organization than with attempting to resolve actual conflicts (Vickers, 1973, p. 153).

Conflict is handled by means of 'rule and role'. Rules are practices and conventions that are accepted by both sides. Roles are a set of expectations that are held by and about an individual. New bureaucratic procedures produce managerial rules that do not match traditional roles. Now where roles are undermined—together with the status that accompanies them—the stability and morale of an organization are put at risk. Rules must be mutually acceptable and agreed. Roles must be accepted and affirmed. Communication between higher and lower levels of an organization is most productive and beneficial when it takes the form of information, advice and interest, rather than the form of directives and binding requirements. Only then will people give of their best: initiative will flourish and output will be sustained.

These serious reservations about the progress of centralized bureaucracy within the Church are reinforced by Dorothy Emmet's distinction (1966, pp. 186f., 207) between quasi-mechanistic organizations where effectiveness is achieved by every human component functioning in a highly predictable way, and where the element of contingency and therefore of human initiative is minimal (say, a conveyor-belt production system or a highly organized city-wide milk-delivery service), on the one hand, and vocational organizations where inter-personal rapport and individual response are crucial, on the other.

Weber's rational–legal authority means that the person acting in a subordinate role has simply to act according to the rule book. 'The model is that of classical economic man, where rationality consists in always doing what would maximize interests, in this case those of the organization.' Emmet points out that this assumes that there is an optimum solution to every problem, that the alternatives are fully calculable and their respective consequences entirely predictable—in other words, there are measurable indices of success.

But in vocational organizations, of which the Church is paradigmatic, the overall purpose is more elusive and the results difficult to quantify. Such work can only be done creatively, Emmet points out, if people are free to do it largely in their own way, motivated above all by their own internal springs of action. Excess bureaucratization of vocational organizations undermines their *raison d'être*, which is to be free to engage with individual human need at a profound level.

The prime consideration in Christian ministry and mission is not the greater efficiency and further aggrandizement of the Church as an institution, but the temporal and eternal welfare of its members and of those it seeks to invite into its fellowship. As William Temple famously remarked, the Christian Church is the only society that exists for the sake of those who do not belong.

6

Charisma and Spiritual Power

CHARISMATIC AUTHORITY

'The man who possesses *mana*, is the one who knows how to make others obey.' The quality that compels obedience is the same mysterious force that gives wind the ability to blow, fire the ability to burn, and a weapon the ability to kill (Caillois, p. 90). Anthropologists are familiar with charismatic authority—a phenomenon as old as human society itself. However, our third type of authority (Weber, pp. 341ff.) has strong contemporary appeal. Weber defines charisma as 'a certain quality of an individual personality by virtue of which he is set apart from ordinary men and treated as endowed with supernatural, superhuman or at least specifically exceptional qualities' (p. 358). Charismatic authority therefore rests on the devotion accorded to 'the specific and exceptional sanctity, heroism or exemplary character of an individual person and of the normative patterns or order revealed or ordained by him' (p. 328).

Charismatic authority is in conflict with the basis of legitimacy, expressed in status, that undergirds a fully established institutional order. Whereas traditional and bureaucratic authority structures enjoy permanence—they maintain what systems theory calls homeostasis—charismatic authority is inherently unstable. It has no mechanisms for appointment or dismissal, no career structure, no salary scale, no training or qualifications. Charismatic leaders and their immediate followers 'stand outside the ties of this world, outside of routine occupations as well as outside the routine obligations

67

of family life' (Eisenstadt, p. 21). Charismatic authority is thus the antithesis of the everyday, mundane and profane world-order (*Alltag*).

A charismatic leader is a revolutionary. His 'administrative officers' are disciples, bound to him by the same charismatic fervour and by personal loyalty. His followers are those whose need and distress—giving rise to what Erikson has called 'charismatic hunger'—have not been met by the traditional or bureaucratic institutions of society. As Holmberg has written:

> Charismatic leadership in its 'pure' or 'intense' form can be defined as a relation between a leader and his followers characterised by a high degree of emotional and cognitive identification of the followers with the leader and his mission. The emotional attitudes that may characterise other types of leadership are here raised to a pitch of absolute intensity: affection becomes devotion, admiration becomes awe, respect turns into reverence, and the feeling of trust approaches blind faith. The leader can do nothing wrong, everything he says, wishes or prescribes is absolutely true and right as he is considered to be a source of goodness, truth and strength in himself. (Holmberg, pp. 141f.)

Reflecting that it is not unusual for a charismatic leader to be opposed as vehemently as he is supported, Holmberg adds: 'To his opponents he may appear a veritable devil, to his followers a demigod' (pp. 141f.)

Charismatic authority is typified by religious proselytizing and by resort to compulsion, including pressurizing techniques that fall short of the use of actual force. The authority of the charismatic leader is guaranteed by signs and miracles, but, by the same token, it is vulnerable to disconfirmation and then rejection as a result of failure at this level (Weber, p. 360). As Eisenstadt comments: 'The charismatic leader gains and maintains authority solely by proving his strength in life. If he wants to be a prophet, he must perform miracles; if he wants to be a war-lord, he must perform heroic deeds' (Eisenstadt, p. 22). It is indeed the prophet who is the charismatic figure *par excellence*, while the priest is the religious embodiment of traditional authority and the deacon or minister is the religious reflection of bureaucratic society where role is more important than status.

Charismatic authority can be the beneficiary of the destabilization of both traditional and bureaucratic régimes. Talcott Parsons, Weber's editor in the work cited here, has written:

> Any situation where an established institutional order has to a considerable extent become disorganized, where established routines, expectations and symbols are broken up or are under attack is a favorable situation for such a movement. This creates widespread psychological insecurity which in time is susceptible of reintegration in terms of attachment to a charismatic movement. (In Weber, p. 71)

However, charismatic authority tends not to emerge from traditional régimes directly, but through the stage of rational–legal authority which is an attempt to shore up a tottering traditional régime (the stultifying and absurd civil-service procedures satirized in Gogol's novel *Dead Souls*, set in Tsarist Russia, might be a case in point). Under pressure, traditional authority resorts to bureaucratic procedures—inflexible, impersonal forms of administration—the hollow shell of time-honoured structures of relationship. But this reliance on the rational–legal mode creates the conditions for the emergence of charismatic authority.

One might conjecture that, because traditional authority has strong transcendent legitimation, overarched by a sense of the sacred —which bureaucratic authority patently lacks—it lends itself, when threatened by failure or collapse, to the direct usurpation of charismatic authority also, for that too draws upon deep personal and emotional forms of commitment. As Weber puts it: 'The corporate group which is subject to charismatic authority is based on an emotional form of communal relationship [*Gemeinde*]' (p. 36). (Rasputin and the other holy men of Tsarist Russia would be examples.)

Dennis Wrong subsumes Weber's charismatic authority under the broader category of 'personal' authority (Wrong, pp. 60ff.). The basis of personal authority consists in a particular disposition of the individual—love, admiration, friendship or the desire to submit and so absorb, as it were, the dominant qualities of the authoritative person. The authority of the beloved over the lover is the paradigm of personal authority (this connects, of course, with Freud's theory of the leader as the focus of mass libidinal transference). Wrong designates personal authority thus:

> Personal authority might be considered a 'pure' type of authority in which commands are issued and obeyed without

the command giver possessing any coercive powers, transferable resources, special competence, or legitimacy conferred by a community. His or her personal significance to the subject constitutes the sole grounds of the latter's compliance. (p. 60)

THE ROUTINIZATION OF CHARISMA

However, according to Weber, the charismatic authority structure is itself unstable—the intense emotional tone and the risky appeal to signs and wonders cannot be sustained indefinitely. Patterns of expectation, of repetition, of appeal to precedent inevitably emerge. Weber terms this 'the routinization of charisma' (Weber, pp. 363ff.). The charismatic element does not disappear but becomes dissociated from the individual leader and embodied in an objective institutional structure, so that the new holders of authority, the successors, hold it at second remove from the original source of power, by virtue of an institutionally legitimized status or office. Contact with the 'Spirit' is now mediated, and even second-hand. In taking care of a key problem of the charismatic model—the question of succession and continuity—this has the effect of changing the basis and nature of the community. The structure of the charismatic community begins to become integrated with the familial structure of society. Rituals for the transfer of authority and of succession are required. Fiscal organization, with the holding of property and the regular payment of the 'administrative staff', now becomes imperative. The charismatic community will begin to exhibit marked symptoms of the traditional or the bureaucratic community, and may even evolve into one or the other.

To evaluate the relevance of the charismatic authority model to the Christian Church today I want to ask a number of questions. In answering them, it will become apparent that I propose to distinguish between the sociological and the theological sense of charisma. The sociological sense is the one given by Weber and expanded and developed by Parsons and Eisenstadt. The theological sense is bound up with the messiahship of Jesus who is anointed as prophet, priest and king for his redeeming work and who incorporates his faithful people into those offices as they are baptized by one Spirit into one body (1 Corinthians 12.13).

WAS JESUS A CHARISMATIC?

Jesus was clearly a charismatic in the sociological sense. He was exceptional and set apart; endowed with supernatural or superhuman qualities, exceptional sanctity, goodness and wisdom. He attracted and retained his followers not on the basis of traditional legitimacy or status, but by virtue of his innate qualities and the sense of the divine and numinous that emanated from him. Like a true sociological charismatic, Jesus was detached from the everyday concerns and responsibilities of human life. He forsook family and home, just as he taught his followers to do; he had nowhere to lay his head. He made no provision for the future, teaching his disciples not to worry about what they would eat or what they would wear. He undermined social conventions, especially cultic conventions. Though apparently cautious and reserved about his miraculous signs, he did not deny that they testified to his extraordinary source of authority. It is typical of the charismatic that he is opposed as vehemently as he is supported: to his opponents, Jesus had a devil and was guilty of blasphemy.

Jesus' unique charismatic authority challenged the traditional authority of the functionaries of the Jewish cult. He believed that the temple would be destroyed and that the eschatological crisis was at hand. As James Dunn has written: 'Jesus' sense of power was so overwhelming in his consciousness, so manifest in his ministry, that he could reach no other conclusion than that the end-time prophecies were already being fulfilled in his ministry, the kingdom was already present' (Dunn, p. 98). But this emphasis on Jesus' sense of being clothed with the power of the Spirit leads from the sociological sense of charisma to the theological sense. In the Christian understanding we have to move from the purely phenomenological description of charisma to the theological evaluation of it. For Christians, Jesus really was endued with unique charisma and was aware of this. As Dunn puts it:

> Jesus thought of himself as God's son and as anointed by the eschatological Spirit, because in prayer he experienced God as Father and in ministry he experienced a power to heal which he could only understand as the power of the end-time and an inspiration to proclaim a message which he could only understand as the gospel of the end-time. (Dunn, p. 67)

Any claims about Jesus' consciousness and experience are to be handled cautiously—as Dunn well knows—but we cannot avoid speaking of consciousness and experience, for they constitute reality

71

for human beings. Dunn's assertions do not go beyond the evidence. They are made in a tradition of experiential theology inaugurated by Schleiermacher, to whom we shall shortly turn for help in making a constructive statement about the nature of the charisma received by Christians in the Church.

WAS ST PAUL A CHARISMATIC?

Paul's charismatic status is ambiguous. On the one hand, he was conscious of having been singled out for a special mission and of possessing divinely imparted apostolic authority. He was an itinerant preacher and healer, who had renounced earthly ties. He suffered the fierce hostility often meted out to charismatics by the religious establishment. He too believed that this earthly scene was already passing away and that worldly claims to legitimacy would be consumed in the coming judgement. But, on the other hand, there are a number of factors to set against this, factors that have the effect of mitigating Paul's charismatic status:

(a) Paul cannot be a pure charismatic in Weber's sense, for that charisma is self-determining and Paul constantly referred his gifts to a higher source, emphasizing that he was merely the unworthy earthen vessel (Shütz, pp. 266f.). Paul—and the other apostles for that matter—see themselves as the custodians of a tradition and as the representatives of a leader who is still spiritually present (Holmberg, p. 160). They are disciples and followers, not centres of a cult.

(b) Paul resisted the attempts of his followers, particularly at Corinth, to elevate him into a typical charismatic leader. As Barrett writes: 'An apostle, they thought, must be . . . a powerful and imposing person, standing out for all the rights he could possibly claim, performing miracles, and accepting the adulation and support of those whom he was able to impress' (1973, p. 322). Paul deliberately relativized his authority to enable his congregations to exercise their own God-given charisma to judge for themselves and to take responsibility for their communal life without constant apostolic supervision (Holmberg, p. 190).

(c) Though an itinerant preacher, sitting light to all earthly ties, Paul nevertheless practised a manual trade—tentmaking—to support himself, following accepted Jewish practice, and evinced a practical and pragmatic attitude to money. He was socially conservative and traded on his status as a Roman citizen to protect him against persecution. He did not, as far as we know, attempt to attract and retain his own disciples, and at the end he was largely abandoned by his supporters. There was certainly no ongoing Pauline movement.

Altogether—signs and wonders notwithstanding—Paul is not a typical Weberian charismatic. But he is a powerful exponent of the theological charisma given to every Christian, for he teaches that through baptism all have been made to drink of the Spirit and have received a spiritual gift or charisma to be exercised for the benefit of all. As he claims to speak in tongues more than them all, his charisma is greater in degree, but not in kind, than theirs (1 Corinthians 12; 14.18).

WAS NEW TESTAMENT CHRISTIANITY CHARISMATIC?

The early Christians, as Barrett points out, felt themselves to be under the immediate governance of the Holy Spirit which represented the breaking in of the new age of God's Kingdom (1966, pp. 1f.). But there was a recognition that charismatic phenomena, such as exorcism, tongues, prophecy and healing, were by no means unique to the Christian Church. Pneumatic men were a familiar sight outside the Church (Dunn, p. 302). This is precisely why Paul lays such emphasis on rightly identifying the Spirit that Christians have received. It is the Spirit of Christ (Romans 8.9), the Spirit of God's Son (Galatians 4.6), the Spirit that confesses the lordship of Jesus (1 Corinthians 12.3).

Alongside the ecstatic manifestations of the Spirit, there is a striking emphasis on the routine aspects of the charismatic community. Charisma leads not only to tongues and prophecy, but to order (*taxis*), edification (*oikodome*) and service (*diakonia*). Helpers and administrators are listed among the charismatics (1 Corinthians 12.28). There is a concern for the equal distribution of benefits in the appointment of the seven 'deacons' (Acts 6) and for deference to be paid to social conventions, as in the matter of women's veils (1 Corinthians 11). As Shütz insists: 'The religious life has its most profound expression in the concrete, everyday reality of human social life visible in the cultically gathered Church' (Shütz, p. 259).

However, while the sociological model of charisma is heavily qualified in the New Testament, the theological model is dominant. The Church is a Spirit-bearing body, a messianic community, in which the risen Christ dwells by his Spirit. Those baptized into that body share his vocation and endowment to serve God as prophets, priests and kings: prophets to proclaim the wonderful words and deeds of God; priests to offer spiritual sacrifices of prayer and praise and to minister to one another in the name of Christ; kings to take their places in his Kingdom and to participate in the governance of his Church (for extensive treatment of this theme see Avis, 1990, *passim*). As 1 Peter 2.9ff. puts it (and the baptismal context is implied in the conventional language of emergence from darkness to light through the illumination of the Holy Spirit), 'You are a chosen race, a royal priesthood, a holy nation, God's own people, in order that you may proclaim the mighty acts of him who called you out of darkness into his marvellous light'.

In Weber's terms, the originating charisma of the New Testament community—identified with Jesus of Nazareth and portrayed as imparted to his followers when he breathed upon them in the upper room (John 20.22) and in the coming of the Holy Spirit in wind and fire at Pentecost (Acts 2)—has become routinized, trapped in the channels of the everyday, mundane structures of human sociality without which it could not be perpetuated at all. But it is this process of routinization that precisely permits the theological dimension of charisma to emerge with greater clarity.

No theologian has brought this out with such radical perception as Friedrich Schleiermacher, who draws a fundamental distinction between the outward life of the Church (its earthly structures, the channels of routinized charisma, we might say) which is subject to change within the historical process, and the essential inner life of the Church which is constant and unchanging and which Schleiermacher describes in terms of consciousness of God through the mediation of Christ. Just as Christ's unique and perfect God-consciousness is to be deemed the presence of God in him, so the Church's enjoyment of the communication of the perfection and blessedness of Christ is the being of God in it. For the redemptive work of Christ is to 'assume believers into the power of his God-consciousness'—into the 'fellowship of his activity and his life'. Christ's threefold office of prophet, priest and king is perpetuated

74

in the life of the Church, for 'everything essentially belonging to Christ's activity has its reflection and continuation in the Church' (Schleiermacher, pp. 582, 385, 535, 425, 590).

Though Schleiermacher was writing without the benefit of Weber's taxonomy of tradition, bureaucracy and charisma, his use of the notion of Christian consciousness—which is not intended in a trivial psychological sense but as the import of the depth of religious experience—can enrich our understanding of charisma as it brings together the sociological and theological senses. As Christians, our charisma is to be thankfully conscious of our gracious standing before God in union with Christ and our vocation is to serve the Lord as prophets, priests and kings within the inevitable constraints of the historical and social structures that channel all human activity.

SIGNS AND WONDERS

As we have seen, the sociological notion of charisma is identified by—among other things—supernatural power evidenced in the performance of miraculous signs. Now we cannot fail to be aware that a vital strand of contemporary Christianity—the charismatic movement—tends, in its more popular thinking at least, to accept this assumption. The presence of the Holy Spirit in the individual and in the Church will manifest itself in supernatural phenomena: ecstatic utterance in tongues and prophecy, healing and exorcism— and charismatics are not shy of talking about raising the dead (Goldingay (ed.), p. 153). In this, they are doing no more than echoing the language of the Bible which is prolific in its references to 'signs and wonders'.

(A) The phrase 'signs and wonders' is widely used throughout the Old Testament and in every type and stratum of its literature. It is the 'signs and wonders' of God's judgement on Pharaoh that persuade him to let the Israelites go free (Exodus 7.3; cf. 3.20, 4.30) and the theological interpretation that constitutes Deuteronomy exults in these: 'Has God ever attempted to go and take a nation for himself from the midst of another nation, by trials, by signs and wonders, by war, by a mighty hand and an outstretched arm, and by terrifying displays of power, as Yahweh your God did for you in Egypt before your very eyes?' (Deuteronomy 4.34; cf. 7.19; 26.8; 29.3; 34.11). Jeremiah sees these signs and wonders continuing 'to this very day' (Jeremiah 32.20f.), though, as the context makes clear, 'the term is also used more broadly to recall God's redemptive purpose for his covenant people, and to bear testimony to his control of the events of history which is evident in the judgement which has fallen on the nation in the form of the Babylonian captivity and the restoration which God has promised' (Kee, p. 11). In Daniel, God's saving acts are personalized, so to speak: 'He delivers and rescues, he works signs and wonders in heaven and on earth, he who has saved Daniel from the power of the lions' (Daniel 6.27).

Turning to the New Testament, the essential vocabulary of supernatural phenomena is given to us in one of the earliest references: 2 Corinthians 12.12: 'The signs of a true apostle were performed among you with utmost patience, signs [*semeia*] and wonders [*terata*] and mighty works [*dynameis*].' These occur either singly or in various combinations in the epistles, gospels and Acts.

(a) The word *dynameis*, translated 'mighty works' or 'miracles', is never defined in the New Testament. We should not assume that for the evangelists and Paul it carries any connotations of breach of natural law. Their interest is not cosmological but soteriological.

(b) These phenomena are clearly not self-authenticating and may be used for good or ill. Satan and the Beast perform signs and wonders to delude humankind (2 Thessalonians 2.9; Revelation 13.13).

(c) The 'working of miracles' or 'mighty works' (*dynameis*) is given by Paul as one of the gifts of the Spirit (*charismata*) in 1 Corinthians 12.10, 28.

(d) Signs, wonders and miracles or mighty works are regarded by Paul, Luke (if Luke was the author of Acts) and the author of Hebrews as the authentic badges of apostleship (1 Corinthians 15.15ff.; 2 Corinthians 12.12; Acts 2.43; 4.30; 5.12; 6.8; 8.13; 14.3; 15.12—Stephen, Philip and Barnabas being included; Hebrews 2.4).

(e) There is a marked difference of emphasis in the way the evangelists present the miraculous aspect of the ministry of

Jesus. While these phenomena occupy nearly a third of Mark's gospel—and nearly a half up to the point where Jerusalem is reached (Evans, p. 27), they are presented in a highly ambiguous way—often furtive and hushed up (Mark 1.25, 34, 44; 3.12; 8.30; 9.9). Luke, on the other hand, glories in 'signs and wonders' and uses the phrase repeatedly and uncritically. As Dunn comments, 'His attitude seems to be: the more eye-catching the miracle the greater the propaganda value' (Dunn, p. 167). Dunn accuses Luke of being interested only in the 'grosser, more physical and tangible expressions of spiritual power' (Dunn, p. 191).

(f) While Mark represents the witnesses of Jesus' ministry as ascribing miracles or mighty works to him (Mark 6.2, 5, 14), there is only one place in the gospels where Jesus himself describes his ministry in terms of 'mighty works [*dynameis*]' (Matthew 11.21, 23; cf. Luke 10.13).

(g) While Jesus is credited with nature miracles and raising the dead, it is Dunn's view that these belong to later strata of the tradition. 'No instances of healing purely physical injuries or mending broken limbs are attributed to Jesus in the earliest stratum of tradition—that is to say, there is no instance of a healing miracle which falls clearly outside the general category of psychosomatic illnesses' (Dunn, p. 71).

(B) We need to set the biblical phenomena against the background of the scientific and cosmological assumptions of the time. Here there are three factors to bear in mind.

(a) We can distinguish, as Kee does, between medicine, miracle and magic. Medicine seeks healing in the natural order, miracle in the divine order, and magic in an occult order (cf. Kee, pp. 126f.). The practice of medicine in the ancient world, though severely handicapped by lack of scientific assumptions, methods and tools, was basically rational. Galen (second century AD), for example, 'believed that he was operating within the realm of reason, so that the therapeutic process would produce predictable results' (Kee, p. 62). Kee adds that 'There is in Galen's writings no significant place for magic, with its assumption that secret techniques will force the hidden powers to act in the desired ways' (ibid.). But the gospels are just not interested in the medical aspects of the healings of Jesus. They are only concerned to show that divine power was at work in the ministry of Jesus.

(b)   The ministry of Jesus in healing and exorcism should be seen in the context of itinerant healers and exorcists of the time. There was nothing unique about this ministry—any more than the phenomena of glossolalia, prophecy, healing and exorcism described by Paul in 1 Corinthians 12 and 14 were unique to the New Testament community. These are 'natural' phenomena, universally attested—innate created capacities of humankind that can be activated or triggered in certain circumstances and under certain spiritual conditions (see Avis, 1990, ch. 8). In the gospels we impinge on the strange world where ancient medicine, primitive magic and spiritual power meet. The telling details of the gospel narrative have the ring of authenticity. As Evans writes:

In the gospels we are far removed from the farrago of recipes and spells, formulae and incantations, and the strings of outlandish words which occur in [the Egyptian magical papyri], but there are also close similarities which are not to be minimized or ignored, for they give a precision to actions and words in the gospels which is concealed in the English versions. (Evans, p. 30)

Evans points in illustration to healing by touching the healer or his garments (Mark 3.10; 5.27–32; 6.56), to innate healing power flowing from healer to recipient like a substance (Mark 5.30) and from healer to assistants (Mark 3.15; 6.7, 13), to healing by applying saliva to the tongue or eyes (Mark 7.33; 8.23), and to touch effecting an immediate cure (Mark 1.31, 41; 5.41; 8.25). The charismatics of today might well ask themselves when they last applied spittle or allowed the sick to touch the hem of their anoraks. The uniqueness of the miraculous healings of Jesus lies not in their taking place, but in the fact that they were directed at the unworthy, the impure, the outcasts, so that all flesh should see the salvation of God (cf. Kee, pp. 78f.).

(c)   We cannot expect the evangelists and other biblical authors to be governed by modern standards of historical evidence and scientific rationality. Though the ancient world was by no means entirely devoid of the scientific approach to such phenomena as disease and healing, it was nevertheless thoroughly imbued with credulity, superstition and a wholesale disregard for scientific methods of collecting and evaluating evidence. The early Christians took literally the more extravagant phenomena of the Old Testament record. For them, these events were no more mysterious than what seemed to them the miracles and mysteries of nature all around them. They were baffled by the movement of the tides, the migration of birds, the causes of lightning, thunder and rain. They could not account for the phases of the moon and did not know what lay beyond the sea. The spontaneous generation of snakes from human corpses and the parthenogenesis of vultures were widely credited. Augustine is unsure whether Apuleius's changing into an ass and back again in *The Golden Ass* is fact or fiction (see Grant). Pliny the Elder, though sceptical of medical charlatanry, is convinced that a reliable prophylactic against miscarriage is an amulet of gazelle leather containing white flesh from a hyena's breast, seven hairs from a hyena and the genital organ of a stag (Kee, p. 8). There is no reason to think that the mind-set of the evangelists was very different. And it will be salutary to bear this and the previous points in mind as we turn now to consider the present-day interest in signs and wonders.

(C) While the charismatic movement as a whole has given prominence to what might be called the ecstatic gifts—tongues, interpretation and prophecy—in *worship*, certain strains within the movement have emphasized the more dynamic phenomena of healing—exorcism and miraculous words of knowledge—in *evangelism* (cf. Gunstone). The claim to engage in 'power evangelism' by John Wimber and his associates and admirers presumably echoes Paul's boast in Romans 15.15–20 that Christ had worked through him to win obedience from the Gentiles 'by word and deed, by the power of signs and wonders, by the power of the Holy Spirit'. The quest for 'power' represents the aspirations of many ordinary Christian folk who have been influenced by the charismatic movement. Without pouring cold water on the longing of many Christians to become more effective instruments of the Spirit of Christ, there are nevertheless some searching observations that need to be made about the 'power' scenario.

(a) The implications of highlighting 'power' in this way are twofold. First, there is a frank assumption that the experience of 'power' is the answer to the needs of the Church and the world: if our evangelism were with 'power', it is supposed, the weakness and decline of the Church would be overcome, militant anti-Christian ideologies would be beaten back, the world would be won for Christ! Secondly, it is hard to escape the conclusion, on these premises, that while these manifestations of 'power' are merely local and limited, and the great breakthrough we long for does not happen, the cause must lie within ourselves. By our sin or unbelief we are, in effect, erecting a barrier to the full flow of the power of the Spirit. Meanwhile, of course, enormous prestige and authority accrues to those whose faith and holiness are such that they have become the unrestricted channels of the Spirit's power.

(b) It is striking that claims to spiritual power and to possession of miraculous gifts today are confined to the tamer varieties of those found in the Bible. In the Old Testament, the power of Yahweh was displayed through the sun (in modern cosmology, the earth) standing still, the sea parting its waves, rivers turning to blood, plagues of frogs, flies and locusts, and the wiping out of a generation of Egyptian first-born sons by the word of the Lord at the hands of his prophet Moses. 'He it was who smote the first-born of Egypt, both of man and of beast; who in thy midst, O Egypt, sent signs and wonders against Pharaoh and all his servants' (Psalm 135.8–9). Miraculous feedings on a vast scale occur in both the Old Testament and the gospels. Chastisement with blindness is a divine judgement in the Old Testament and the New (2 Kings 6.18; Acts 13.11). Striking with leprosy is found in 2 Kings 5.27 and making dumb in Luke 1.20. Striking dead at the authority of the apostles (Acts 5.1–11) is a pale imitation of the scale of judgement by death in the Pentateuch. Nature miracles, especially with water, are plentiful in the Old Testament and the gospels. Immunity to poisonous snake bites was provided by divine power when Moses lifted up the brazen serpent in the wilderness and when Paul shook off the snake that had fastened on him into the fire (Numbers 21.9; Acts 28.3–6). The early Christians expected immunity both from poisonous snake bites and from poisoned chalices (Mark 16.18). Miraculous transportation in the Spirit was provided for Philip (Acts 8.39–40) and the prison doors were miraculously opened for Peter and other apostles more than once (Acts 5.19; 12.7–10).

Most of these are not part of the repertoire of today's 'power evangelists'! Their ministry is evidently to bring the power of the Spirit to bear on the lives and hearts of individuals—the natural elements are a tougher proposition! The snake-handlers of the Dolley-Pond-Church-of-God-With-Signs-Following, Tennessee, are not typical! On the evidence of scripture, the power of the Spirit was manifested in biblical times in ways that we do not expect to see today. If our evangelists were able to feed the hungry millions in Africa, or cure AIDS sufferers, the credibility of the Christian gospel would be beyond question. However, if they were able to pronounce supernatural sentence of judgement by death or disease, the civil authorities might have something to say about it!

(c) The blatant discrepancy between biblical signs and wonders and those claimed by some today raises the probability that not all the biblical narratives are to be taken literally. Without questioning the reality of mighty acts of God in history, many theologians would see these as being accomplished through human co-operation and resources when these are offered up to God. And biblical scholars would accept that ancient sagas of God's dealings with his people have become expanded, embroidered and reinterpreted, as well as assimilating legendary material. For example, few intellectually and morally alert readers of the Exodus narrative would take the plagues, the death of the first-born, the parting of the Red Sea and the divine command to exterminate the Canaanites—men, women, children and animals—at face value. They would tend to find the theological significance of the story in Yahweh's bringing a demoralized, oppressed multitude into a covenant relation with himself, enabling them to find their true identity as

81

the servant nation of the Lord, and leading them, through the human agency of Moses and Aaron, safely through many dangers to a land where they could offer worship to their God and delight to regulate their lives by his laws.

The Old Testament calls for an effort of discrimination and interpretation, bringing to bear our knowledge of the natural world and of the history and social behaviour of humankind. We also need to be fully alert to what our moral conscience tells us about the implications of some of the more bloodthirsty and gruesome aspects of these stories for our understanding of the character of God. A similar act of interpretation is demanded by the nature of the New Testament literature, which scholarship reveals to have passed through many stages, oral and written, and to have been subject to many competing influences, not least the demands of the early Christian communities for answers to their questions, legitimation of practices that they found convenient, and morale-boosting in the face of their enemies. However, it also follows that contemporary claims to the power of the Spirit, manifested in signs and wonders, must be subjected to a process of impartial and informed evaluation.

SPIRITUAL POWER

In a world where power is measured by armed might, financial muscle, and in the ability to appeal to people's baser instincts through the mass media, it is all too easy for Christians to hanker after a form of power that produces empirically measurable results—instantaneous healings, overpowering spiritual conviction with emotional manifestations, apparently inexplicable gifts of knowledge, and other forms of knock-down evidence for a spiritual reality from beyond this world yet impinging manifestly upon it. This understandable thirst for signs and wonders savours, however, of the temptation Jesus rejected in the desert when he turned his back on bread and circuses and embraced the way of obscurity, humility, suffering, rejection and death. For Paul, fellowship in Christ's suffering was the condition for experiencing the power of his resurrection (Philippians 3.10).

The power of Jesus Christ was revealed not chiefly in signs and wonders—these were often somewhat furtive and hushed up, as we have seen—but in this twofold authority: first, of his moral character with its selfless compassion and unsullied goodness, and second, of the truth of his teaching as the gospel of God. The Church today is called to the imitation of Christ in these two respects—to reflect his righteousness and proclaim his truth. Then it will find that it does indeed have power—or, rather, authority. It will not allow itself to be marginalized or silenced. It will not glory in its ineffectiveness, for that would be to collude with an unbelieving world in giving legitimation to the decline of the Church. But it will glory in the cross of Christ for *that* is the power of God unto salvation for everyone who has faith (Romans 1.16). Like Paul, it will want to know nothing 'except Jesus Christ and him crucified', so that its *message* may be 'in demonstration of the Spirit and of power' (1 Corinthians 2.2, 4).

The distinctive charisma of the Christian life is found in identification with Christ's way of self-emptying, self-sacrifice, suffering in solidarity with all victims of human hurt or natural affliction, and self-oblation to the will of the Father. For out of that will come the self-evidencing authority of justice, truth and love. Ultimately, the power that the Spirit gives is the power of love. It was as they beheld his wounds that the risen Christ breathed his Spirit upon his disciples (John 20.20–22).

7

Open Society: Open Church

THE CHURCH AS AN 'OPEN SOCIETY'?

During the darkest years of the Second World War, Karl Popper was writing his massive diatribe *The Open Society and its Enemies*. Isolated from the conflict—and from academic resources —in New Zealand, Popper regarded *The Open Society* (together with *The Poverty of Historicism*) as his contribution to the Allied war effort. He singled out Plato, Hegel and Marx as theorists of totalitarian tyranny. It has been Popper's life's work to maintain the principle of open, critical discussion as the basis of both a democratic society and the scientific community.

Popper derives the notions of the open society and the closed society from Henri Bergson's *The Two Sources of Morality and Religion* (French original 1032) and acknowledges the debt (1966, I, p. 202). Bergson had developed a fundamental contrast between two archetypal forms of society, religion and morality. The closed society was instinctive and 'natural' like an ant-hill, legitimated by 'static' religion functioning in the realm of myth and by 'static' morality based on the sense of obligation. The open society, on the other hand, transcended its instinctive and natural origins and attained to a sense of 'humanity'. It was informed by 'dynamic' religion arising from individual mysticism, a sense of the transcendent sacred. Its morality was 'dynamic' and based not on mere obligation, but on a creative response to the situation (Bergson, pp. 266ff., 211ff., 220f.). Popper is at pains to point out that, while Bergson attributes the transition from a closed to an open society to mysticism, for him mysticism represents a longing for the lost unity of the closed society and the transition is attributable to the emergence of rational criticism (1966, I, p. 202). (Both thinkers are agreed, however, that the open society only becomes possible when individuals begin to transcend the mass.) It is an important distinction—and one relevant to our ultimate purpose—that while for Bergson mysticism and a sense of the sacred bring deliverance from the closed society, for Popper mysticism is precisely the power behind it. It is the enemy of the free society. A society imbued with the sacred, overarched by a sacred canopy, can never tolerate criticism or change. It is undergirded by magic and ruled by taboos. Only when the sacral nature of society is challenged can a free society be born:

> The transition takes place when social institutions are first consciously recognised as man-made, and when their conscious alteration is discussed in terms of their suitability for the achievement of human aims or purposes. . . . The closed society breaks down when the supernatural awe with which the social order is considered gives way to active interference and to the conscious pursuit of personal or group interests. (1966, I, p. 294)

The Christian Church is traditionally (and still today in Roman Catholicism and Orthodoxy) a closed society, claiming to be the embodiment of the sacred, reinforced with various taboos, especially those relating to women and sex. Study of the psychological and sociological dynamics of religion suggests that religion is a human production; specifically, that the Christian religion is a human response (though a response to a genuinely 'other' divine reality), and that the Church as a social institution is (to use Popper's phrase) man-made. Once that is recognized, the stage is set for the transition to an 'open society' in the Church and the removal of magical, irrational, and man-made taboos affecting women and sexual life. The consequences for the Roman Catholic Church and the Orthodox Churches would be revolutionary; for the Anglican Church and other reformed Churches less so. But for all traditions, learning from the sciences of the human world would lead to a more human Church.

Popper singles out several characteristics of the closed society as delineated particularly by Plato in *The Laws*. First, the closed society fosters an attitude of total dependence on the leadership, resulting in passivity, docility and lack of initiative. As Plato writes:

No one, man or woman, must ever be left without someone in charge of him; nobody must get into the habit of acting alone and independently . . . and in peace and war alike we must give our constant attention and obedience to our leader, submitting to his guidance even in tiny details. . . . We must condition ourselves to an instinctive rejection of the very notion of doing anything without our companions; we must live a life in which we never do anything if possible, except by combined and united action as members of a group. . . . This is what we must practise in peacetime, right from childhood— the exercise of authority over others and submission to them in turn. (Plato, p. 48)

Altogether, Plato insists, in the ideal society 'freedom from control must be uncompromisingly eliminated' (ibid.). In traditional Catholicism, we find a comparable situation. As Solignac has pointed out, infantile, passive attitudes or 'oral' dependency are systematically inculcated. Dostoyevsky's Grand Inquisitor informs the Lord: 'We have corrected your great work and have based it on miracle, mystery and authority. And men rejoiced that they were once more led like sheep and that the terrible gift which had brought them so much suffering had at last been lifted from their hearts' (I, p. 301).

Modern theory of management regards this sort of remorseless supervision as destructive. Strong predictability within an institution is bought at the price of efficiency. To be effective, an organization has to tolerate a high degree of unpredictability as the condition for devolving responsibility and encouraging initiative:

Attempts to monitor what every subordinate is doing all the time tend to be counterproductive; attempts to make the activity of others predictable may routinize, suppress intelligence and flexibility and turn the energies of subordinates to frustrating the projects of at least some of their superiors. (MacIntyre, pp. 100f.)

Communication there must be, but it should take the form of advice, information and interest, not of instructions, decisions and requirements.

Secondly, since the society is sacred (like the Church) or a reflection of ideal forms (as in Plato), the well-being of the society becomes the criterion of good and evil (Popper, 1966, I, p. 107).

Morality becomes a function of the interests of the society or state. Ends will justify means. Casuistry will flourish. Double-truths will be found convenient. The description is a familiar one to Church historians and students of ecclesiastical politics!

Thirdly, the closed society will be governed by its elders; its ruling college will necessarily be of mature years. Plato's reasoning here is explicit and ingenuous: the society is sacred, perfect, the embodiment of a divine purpose; therefore it does not need to change; therefore let it be ruled by those who are most set in their ways and inflexible in their thinking: let the elders preside (Popper, 1966, I, pp. 133f.). Once again, the description strikes rather too close to home. In the Latin tradition, the rule of the elders acquired a subtler basis. As Hannah Arendt points out, the Romans regarded their elders as grown close to the past and to the founding fathers of their civilization. One grew towards the past, not the future. Tradition, in the stewardship of the elders, was the sanctification of the past, and permanence the attribute of the sacred (Arendt, pp. 123f.). This is the concept of authority that underlies pre-Enlightenment Western civilization and continues to inform traditional ecclesiology. Bertrand Russell commented, in his study of *Power*, on 'the feebleness and slowness of movement, analogous to that of old men, which is often seen in old organizations' in which the tyranny of centuries of habit can become the cause of collapse (B. Russell, p. 183). There are few institutions, still extant, older than the Christian Church!

Fourthly, the 'closed' society will be governed in the light of revelation. Plato's philosopher-ruler is not merely a seeker after wisdom like Socrates (as Popper underlines), but claims to be its possessor. He is one who enjoys intellectual perception of the ideal world of Forms and is compelled to translate his vision into actuality on earth (Popper, 1966, I, pp. 144f.). So too the traditional Church has boldly claimed to speak with divine authority, to have the mind of Christ, to be led by the Holy Spirit. And this not merely in the acceptable sense that through prayer, study and self-discipline it humbly seeks divine guidance and trusts that in some measure it has it; but in the unacceptable hubristic sense that it claims to point to guarantees that it has it, and claims infallibility for its decrees or the guidance of the Spirit for particular pieces of legislation, with the corollary and consequence that those who question or resist such decrees or canon laws are to be regarded as of 'another spirit' and to be treated accordingly. As we have already observed, the 'closed' society is immersed in its collective subjectivity. It cannot stand outside itself, as it were, and make an objective judgement. It lacks self-transcendence. Its sacred legitimation and magical taboos depend on a failure to distinguish between custom, convention and tradition on the one hand, and nature, truth or the will of God on the other. The two are merged and critical discrimination is inhibited (1966, I, p. 172).

It is Popper's claim that the transition from the closed to the open society must be judged to be 'one of the deepest revolutions through which mankind has passed' (1966, I, p. 175). Liberal, tolerant, democratic values hold out the best hope for the future of mankind. Collectivism is blind. Individualism is enlightened. Closed thinking cannot make the changes necessary to survive. Open criticism may come up with the answers to unforeseen problems. Psychological research reveals that it is creative, innovative people who can stand the strain of cognitive dissonance, intellectual tension, unresolved problems. They are the ones who are going to solve those problems if anyone is. Progress requires liberty (cf. Storr, pp. 237f., 279f.).

An essential aspect of that freedom is openness to discussion and criticism. The sociologist Hugh Dalziel Duncan has pointed out that, now that authority needs to be justified and is no longer self-authenticating, an openness to criticism both within an institution's borders and across its frontiers is the *sine qua non* of authority:

> Only when criticism is open, free, informed, and widely communicated, when it is an integral part of institutional structure, and it is communicated *without*, among various publics, as well as *within* the private public of the institution, can there be authority based on reason in society. (Duncan, p. 288)

Once society has undergone that revolution, there can be no permanent return to the totalitarian conditions of the closed society. Of course we are aware (though Popper himself could be clearer about this) that the open society has its legitimations too, the secular world has its own version of 'the sacred canopy'. There can be no society in which 'anything goes' and 'nothing is sacred'. But that is a challenge to work out a conception of authority that respects freedom of thought and criticism without giving reign to rampant individualism and antisocial behaviour. But Popper is surely right to deprive us of any illusions that a return to the comforting, secure, enveloping, maternal womb-like closed society is possible. There is a point of no return. Popper's religious imagery here makes it unnecessary for me to point out the moral for the benefit of the Church:

> We can never return to the alleged innocence and beauty of the closed society. Our dream of heaven cannot be realised on earth. . . . For those who have eaten of the tree of knowledge, paradise is lost. . . . If we dream of a return to our childhood, if we are tempted to rely on others and so be happy, if we shrink from the task of carrying our cross, the cross of humaneness, of reason, of responsibility, if we lose courage and flinch from the strain, then we must try to fortify ourselves with a clear understanding of the decision before us. . . . If we wish to remain human, then there is only one way, the way into the open society. (1966, I, pp. 200f.)

THE DIALECTICAL PURSUIT OF TRUTH

The greatest compliment that one can pay to a 'truth' is to criticize it. Criticism of truth means taking it seriously and taking God seriously, for only in God is ultimate truth—'the truth, the whole truth and nothing but the truth'—to be found. Truth is a transcendent category that relativizes all our human convictions, however hallowed by tradition. Truth is the perfect accord of the knowing mind with objective reality—and that is a consummation not vouchsafed us in this life where, even in our moments of clearest vision, we still 'see through a glass darkly'.

On the other hand, to attempt to protect a 'truth' from criticism by censorship is to idolize what is human, finite and limited. Even on a strong view of divine revelation, God's truth has to be put into human words—clothed in the garments of creaturely reality, as Barth insisted. Those human words can never be fully commensurate with the divine Word. To absolutize a given 'truth' is therefore not to serve the truth at all, but rather to 'suppress the truth in unrighteousness'.

To criticize the truth, then, is to engage profoundly with the truth, to appropriate it, wrestle with it, strive to master it—or, better still, to allow it to master us. Truth demands a response not merely at the level of theory, but at the level of praxis. We must make trial of the truth, and as we do so—provided it is indeed the truth of God—it will make trial of us. It is incompatible with the nature of truth for it to be received passively. 'Truth is subjectivity' (Kierkegaard). We can only know it for the truth that it is when it thrusts itself upon us and claims our assent. As we test its credentials through rigorous criticism, evaluation and appreciation, it becomes a living part of us. Jacob wrestled with the angel and the angel overthrew him. But as Jacob went limping on his way, he carried a blessing with him (Genesis 32.22ff.).

Nietzsche captured the attitude of the ideal disciple to the master's teaching:

> When he had said that, his disciple shouted. . . 'But I believe
> in your cause and consider it so strong that I shall say every-
> thing, everything that I can find in my heart to say against it.'
> The Innovator laughed. . . 'This kind of discipleship', he said
> then, 'is the best.' (Kaufman, 1968, p. 116)

It would be anachronistic to call this Popperian, but it can serve as a motto for Popper's programme where rationality consists in open-ness to rational criticism.

In the context of its author's biography, Popper's concept of the open society represents the broad social and political application of his theory of scientific method. For Popper, the original and arche-typal open society is the scientific community, which—ideally—functions in an open, self-critical and self-correcting way. Scientific discovery, according to Popper, operates by a twofold method of 'conjecture and refutation', of devising theories and then attempting to smash them. Scientific work is bold, imaginative and wasteful. It is not afraid to make mistakes: that is how it learns. As Popper insists: 'Every discovery of a mistake constitutes a real advance in our know-ledge' (1966, II, p. 376). Popper would agree with Whitehead that 'Panic of error is the death of progress' (Whitehead, p. 222). There is a dialectical pattern here: conjecture and refutation, trial and error, theory and practice, speculation and falsification. (It was Hegel who said 'What is most harmful is trying to preserve oneself from errors' (Kaufman, 1965, p. 170).) Development, advance, comes only through conflict. That is why Popper insists on throwing open the doors to all comers: every suggestion, every source, whether it be tradition, reason, imagination or observation, is welcome. But, Popper crucially points out, 'none has any authority' and nothing is exempt from criticism (1963, p. 27; 1966, II, p. 378).

Popper's great treatise on scientific method was entitled *The Logic of Scientific Discovery*. The word 'logic' is important, for

Popper's broadly open and critical approach is also supported by a maverick philosopher of science, Paul Feyerabend, for whom even logic is not sacrosanct. Feyerabend, a self-styled 'epistemological anarchist', adopts the slogan 'anything goes'. Science is an intellectual adventure that knows no limits and is bound by no rules—'not even the rules of logic'. Unlike Popper, Feyerabend is no rationalist: for him nothing is ever settled, everything remains in the melting pot, there is no convergence, no advance of science, no assured results. Chaos is itself creative (Feyerabend, pp. 18, 67, 182, 30). As I have suggested elsewhere (1986b, p. 203), this description bears an unnerving resemblance to Christian theology with its chronic dearth of firm conclusions. But it does not follow that in theology, any more than in science, we are merely groping in the dark, without knowledge and with nothing to go by. In both disciplines we are exploring at the limits of human perception. Our language is analogical and symbolic. Our ideologies set up a smoke screen between ourselves and the object of enquiry. Our best insights or theories are stabs of light in the darkness; the world they illuminate shades off on all sides into mystery. In theology, the most powerful source of illumination is the light of the knowledge of the glory of God that shines in the face of Jesus Christ (2 Corinthians 4.6).

Popper (but not Feyerabend) is stoutly in the tradition of John Stuart Mill, and much of what he says about openness, liberty and criticism reads like a paraphrase of Mill's *On Liberty*. Mill even has the principle of falsification: 'There is the greatest difference', he points out, 'between presuming an opinion to be true because, with every opportunity for contesting it, it has not been refuted, and assuming its truth for the purpose of not permitting its refutation. Complete liberty of contradicting and disproving our opinion is the very condition which justifies us in assuming its truth.' Our best-founded convictions 'have no safeguard to rest on but a standing invitation to the whole world to prove them unfounded'. Open discussion and criticism are therefore imperative. Popularly held views seldom represent the whole truth: heretical opinions often preserve vital corrective insights that have been suppressed; it is essential that they be heard. 'All silencing of discussion is an assumption of infallibility' (Mill, pp. 79, 81, 108, 77). Mill even implies a notion of polarity when he writes: 'Truth, in the great practical concerns of life, is so much a question of the reconciling and combining of opposites that very few have minds sufficiently capacious and impartial to make the adjustment with an approach to

91

correctness, and it has to be made by the rough process of a struggle between combatants fighting under hostile banners' (pp. 110f.).

Though Popper and Mill talk like Enlightenment rationalists with their emphasis on cool reason, logic and attainable truth, the upshot of their views is something different: a radical pluralism of human ends and values. In his essay on Mill, Isaiah Berlin has pointed out that Mill's argument was plausible on the assumption (whether Mill was consciously aware of it or not) that 'human knowledge was in principle never complete, and always fallible; that there was no single, universally visible, truth; that each man, each nation, each civilisation might take its own road towards its own goal'; that there is no unchanging human nature and no single solution to its diverse problems. The rationalist assumption of the Enlightenment, that there is a single discoverable truth, a common end for mankind and but one way of attaining it, does not describe the modern pluralistic world; it does not speak to our condition. Rationalistic monism in any form—secular or religious—can only be a totalitarian threat to human liberty. The possibility of diversity, collision and tragic conflict cannot be eliminated: they are part and parcel of the predicament of humankind. What is needed, Berlin insists, is not—as we are so often told by political or religious pundits—more belief, stronger leadership and a more scientific organization of our society, but rather the opposite: 'less Messianic ardour, more enlightened scepticism, more toleration of idiosyncrasies, . . . more room for the attainment of their personal ends by individuals and by minorities'. Berlin expresses a preference for 'the wicked Tallyrand's *surtout pas trop de zèle*' and believes it to be more humane than the puritanical Robespierre's demand for virtuous uniformity. Authority is not infallible but merely expedient. 'Since no solution can be guaranteed against error, no disposition is final.' Berlin therefore advocates 'a loose texture and toleration of a minimum of inefficiency, even a degree of indulgence in idle talk, idle curiosity, aimless pursuit of this or that without authorisation—"conspicuous waste" itself'—as the best guarantee of individual happiness and the only condition conducive to the truth coming to light (Berlin, pp. 188, 39f.; cf. 154, 169ff.).

In adducing the views of Feyerabend and Berlin, we have been moderating the Popperian ideal of cool, disinterested logic and remorseless dispassionate criticism by giving due weight to human interests, ideological complications and the human genius for 'doing one's own thing'. The pursuit of truth surely follows a very meandering path with much lingering on the way, doubling back, losing sight of the destination, and so on. In the realm of science, Popper's iconoclasm is the exception rather than the norm. The scientific community is not unambiguously Popper's open society with no motive but the truth, but is often conservative, traditional, divided into camps, defensive. Its operations are for the most part pedestrian, routine and predictable. T. S. Kuhn's model of the paradigm (or, in his later thought, the 'matrix of discovery' with its authoritative 'exemplars') is more realistic both about individuals and communities. Kuhn is surely right to point to the 'community structure' of science with its psychological and social factors as the key to how science progresses. For Kuhn, it is ideology not reason that is decisive.

However, we need to be aware of the phenomenon of self-fulfilling prophecy in this connection. The picture of scientists compliantly operating within the received paradigms, if widely accepted, could foster an attitude of complacency and timidity. It needs to be said that Kuhn's version is largely *descriptive* and Popper's largely *prescriptive*. As Lakatos has argued, if Kuhn is right, truth lies in consensus, in majorities, in power. For Popper (and Lakatos himself) the truth is transcendent, not embodied in any paradigm, however widely accepted. In place of the concept of the 'foundation' of knowledge, Lakatos advocates the concept of the 'fallible–critical growth' of knowledge (Kuhn; Lakatos and Musgrave (eds); Suppe (ed.)).

It does not require any great stretch of the imagination to see these two opposed views of the growth of knowledge reflected in the Church. Christian doctrines are its paradigms. Most laity, clergy and bishops operate happily within the prevailing paradigms. The Church is not manifestly an open society in which criticism flourishes. It lives by tradition; it is conservative and defensive. Though divided into camps, these do not represent ultimately incompatible paradigms of Christianity. In this scenario, it is the theologians— mostly, but not exclusively, academics in university posts—who represent the Popperian critics. Their vocation is to probe, to test and, where necessary, to reconstruct. They are the first to sense the crumbling of old paradigms and the emergence of new ones. It is their duty not to fall uncritically for these and not to be swayed by ephemeral trends, but to scrutinize them with the same critical rigour that they mete out to traditional views. Corresponding to Kuhn's distinction between 'normal' and 'extraordinary' science are the day-to-day teaching of the Church on the one hand, and the radical, innovatory thinking of theologians on the other.

Roy Bhaskar has highlighted two fallacies to be avoided when we consider the development of knowledge: 'The first is to suppose that science grows but does not change. The second is to suppose that science changes but does not grow' (Bhaskar, p. 190). Applied to theology, the first is the *rationalist fallacy of conservatives*: theology grows but does not essentially change. Conservatives assume that we can go forward in the serene assurance that special providences, miracles, virgin birth, etc., will remain untouched. Dogma expands and consolidates its empire, but its battles are fought once and for all. The second is the *relativist fallacy of liberals*: there is continual movement, but it is a meaningless flux which does not bring us any nearer to the truth. As Newman saw so clearly, relativistic liberalism has a sceptical, pragmatic view of truth. It does not believe that truth is attainable and it does not much care. That is the antithesis of the Popperian approach—in which the pursuit of truth is a fruitful, though arduous, quest, where there are genuine gains to be made.

In reality, however, there is both change and growth. For all the fallibility of our conjectures, certain errors can be ruled out once and for all (this is surely the meaning of dogma), certain gains can be permanently consolidated (this is what is meant by tradition). We do move nearer the light because (as Polanyi might say) it sheds clues that lead us on. It is Polanyi himself who points out that a living tradition generates elements of novelty. It is not the explicit statements of a tradition that provide the dynamic for its continuance, but the clues incorporated in the tacit dimension that are picked up from generation to generation and then may receive varying explicit expression.

> Every process of reinterpretation introduces elements which are wholly novel. . . . A traditional process of creative thought cannot be carried on without wholly new additions being made to existing tradition at every stage of transmission. . . . It is logically impossible for tradition to operate without the addition of wholly original interpretative judgements at every stage of transmission. (Polanyi, p. 44)

Once again, a dialectical pattern is beginning to emerge: tradition and criticism, tenacity and pluralism, orthodoxy and innovation, coherence and openness. All openness is heuristic; all closure is provisional. Without stability we cannot survive; without innovation we cannot progress. Reality is open, continuous and interrelated, but our knowledge of it is limited, discontinuous and marked by relative closure. Speculative contemplation has seen the movements of openness and closure written into the texture of the universe. 'Motion or change and identity or rest', wrote Emerson, 'are the first and second secrets of nature.' 'Star, sand, fire, water, tree, man, it is still one stuff and betrays the same properties'—a finite set of basic geometrical patterns in an infinite number of dynamic variations. At the microcosmic and macrocosmic levels alike, the polarity of openness and closure pertains. There are two fundamental morphological archetypes, writes G. Kepes: 'expression of order, coherence, discipline, stability on the one hand; expression of chaos, movement, vitality, change on the other'. These complementary movements of openness and closure constitute 'the dynamic substance of our universe':

> Wherever we look, we find configurations that are either to be understood as patterns of order, of closure, of a tendency towards a centre, cohesion and balance; or as patterns of mobility, freedom, change or opening. . . . Cosmos and chaos . . . the Apollonian spirit of measure and the Dionysian principle of chaotic life, organisation and randomness, stasis and kinesis . . . all these are different aspects of the same polarity of configuration. (Cited Koestler, p. 389)

Concealed in these speculations, we have the transition from the dialectical pursuit of truth to the structural concept of polarity. But that is a major theme that requires extended discussion on a separate occasion.

8

Learning for Leadership

The Christian Church seems to have been founded without much care for modern management principles. If the twelve apostles had been put through the gamut of aptitude tests and psychological assessment, most would have failed to make the grade. They were, by all accounts, lacking in the right background, education and vocational aptitude. Peter was impulsive and given to rash outbursts. James and John put personal needs before company loyalty—abandoning the fishing business without notice to follow the call of a wandering rabbi. Thomas evinced a sceptical attitude that, in most enterprises, would tend to undermine morale. Matthew would certainly have been blacklisted by any local chamber of commerce. Both James the son of Alphaeus and Thaddaeus had radical leanings and were prone to rock the boat. Only one of the disciples showed considerable management potential: a man of initiative and resourcefulness, with a sharp business mind and useful contacts in high places, Judas Iscariot might have managed successfully the expanding enterprise that began in Nazareth.

If the gospels are any indication, Jesus Christ showed scant regard for modern management wisdom. He was not looking for managers, but for *learners* and *leaders*—disciples and apostles. According to Mark, Jesus appointed the Twelve 'to be with him, and to be sent out to proclaim the message' (Mark 3.14). This fact points towards the twofold requirement of today's Church for (a) highly trained personnel, equipped with professional skills, whose learning programme continues throughout their career, and whose sheer competence will gain them a hearing in a climate that is hostile to all pretensions to authority; and (b) leaders of communities who can not only ensure

96

that all things are done decently and in order (management skills), but who can focus and direct the energies and even the conflicts of that faith community towards the attainment of goals, the overcoming of problems, and the realization of a vision of the glory and grace of God.

Both these attributes, learning and leadership, presuppose management ability, for nothing can be achieved without the orderly marshalling of resources and the efficient running of the organizational machine. That is not at all to be despised, but it will not set the world on fire. Too often, of course, even that necessary minimum is not attained and then learned skills and leadership ability are frustrated. Efficient management in the Church is the bottom line, the *sine qua non*, but, far from being an end in itself, it is simply the launching pad for the Church's mission in which learned skills and leadership flair are given their opportunity.

In this chapter we focus on learning for leadership ('to be with him . . .') before turning in the next two chapters to the substance of leadership ('. . . and to be sent out to proclaim the message'). My thesis in the present chapter is the unfashionable one that *leadership demands outstanding intellectual ability and outstanding intellectual application*.

The leader's essential capacity for focusing on the primary task and presiding over the solving of major problems (to be developed in the next chapter) demands outstanding intellectual performance. In his recent book *The Age of Unreason*, Charles Handy has highlighted the value of sheer intelligence in this age of automation and electronic information processing. Routine tasks can be done for us. What we have to do for ourselves, and what will be in increasing demand and at a premium in the future, is the intelligence to discern needs, to grasp aims, and to solve conceptual problems. A quarter of a century ago, the American authors of *The Social Psychology of Organizations* were warning that the intellectual aspect of leadership had been neglected:

> Persuasiveness, warmth and interpersonal skills are frequently urged as the essentials of leadership, but to what end? If a leader is seriously mistaken about the systemic requirements of his organization, his interpersonal abilities may become organizational liabilities. (Katz and Kahn, p. 313)

The higher we go up the echelons of an organization, the more conceptual skills outshine technical and inter-personal skills (p. 314).

A question for all institutions is whether rising through the ranks is the best preparation for leadership at the top. Are the required qualities the same? Before he became a globe-trotting trouble-shooter and international pundit, Henry Kissinger argued that they were not. One of the paradoxes of an increasingly specialized and bureaucratic society, he pointed out, was that 'the qualities rewarded in the rise to eminence are less and less the qualities required once eminence is reached':

> Specialization encourages administrative and technical skills, which are not necessarily related to the vision and creativity needed for leadership. The essence of good administration is coordination among the specialized functions of a bureaucracy. The task of the executive is to infuse and occasionally to transcend routine with purpose. (in Bennis *et al.* (eds), p. 436)

What does this say about the wisdom of the practice, common in the Church, of drawing bishops from those who have proved their value in administration—as archdeacons, officers of boards, or principals of theological colleges? It suggests that success in these largely administrative offices is not in itself a sufficient indication of leadership ability.

Before we can be leaders we must be learners. In an age that is sceptical of all pretensions to authority, any credible form of leadership must be able to demonstrate competence. Claims to exercise authority, without demonstrable competence to do so, will soon be shot to pieces. The hollowness of unqualified leadership was already mocked by Shakespeare:

> Man, proud man,
> Drest in a little brief authority,
> Most ignorant of what he's most assured.
> *(Measure for Measure*, II, ii, 117ff.)

Modern writers on authority, having struggled through the quick-sands of traditional, hierarchical forms of authority, seem to feel that they have gained a firm foothold when they come to discuss the authority of competence. Wrong defines this as 'a power relation in which the subject obeys the directives of the authority out of belief in the authority's superior competence or expertise to decide which actions will best serve the subject's interests and goals' (Wrong, p. 53). The focus on competence allows us to bring out the rational nature of authority, in that it rests on the ability to issue directions that are capable of rational elaboration. Authoritative communications 'possess the potentiality of reasoned elaboration—

they are "worthy of acceptance"' (Friedrich, pp. 29, 32).

This view of authority is acutely relevant to the Church, which exerts leadership in the realm of action—morals, behaviour and socio-political involvement—but also in the realm of truth: in its teaching ministry, it holds out what is to be believed by the faithful. Now, as Yves Simon has pointed out, when the issue is one of truth, the person in authority has the character of a witness, testifying to realities of which he is informed and to which he directs the credence of his hearers (Y. Simon, p. 84). Of course, mere competence is not a sufficient condition for exercising authority, for there are no doubt many competent people who are not entrusted with an authoritative role (Shütz, pp. 9ff.), but it is certainly a necessary condition.

However, it may be argued that this stress on competence is irrelevant to leadership, because leadership is a gift. Either you are born with it or you are not. True, it can be developed and strengthened, but you have to have it in you to start with. There is something to be said for this point of view: there are some individuals who will never lead in any circumstances because they are not assertive enough. They just have not got what it takes. But it is striking that writers on leadership and management today insist with one voice that leaders are made not born, and that leadership is elicited by the situation. As Rice has put it: 'Two heroes die hard in our culture: the gifted amateur and the born leader' (1965, p. 24). Altogether, while it is undeniable that leadership requires outstanding intellectual ability, it also demands outstanding intellectual application. It is in tune with modern leadership and management philosophy and research to insist that the Church must give priority to providing leaders of intellectual calibre—highly trained personnel, equipped with professional skills which they will continue to develop throughout their careers, and whose sheer competence will gain them a hearing in a hostile environment.

How adequately are the Churches responding to this imperative? Each must answer for itself. As far as my own Church—the Church of England—is concerned, there seems to be little cause for complacency and some cause for concern.

A series of publications has exposed the lack of intellectual and theological rigour in Anglican thought in England. More than thirty years ago, in the volume *Essays in Anglican Self-Criticism* (ed. Paton), Denys Munby delivered a scathing critique of the shortcomings of Anglican pronouncements on social and economic questions. He spoke of the 'ineptitude' and 'barrenness' of Christian sociology which could produce nothing better than 'pompous platitudes, academic clichés which cannot be given any concrete application, or statements whose folly is immediately obvious to any expert in the field in question'. Munby concluded that it was 'exceedingly rare that one can find sound theological insight unadulterated with economic nonsense' in Anglican writing on society (Paton (ed.), pp. 53ff., 58). While individual Anglican theologians no longer generally invite such criticism, the reports of synods and other bodies not infrequently still lay themselves open to the retort that their recommendations fail to make economic or political sense.

The contributors to a recent symposium on the role of the Church of England today (ed. Moyser) are unanimous about one thing: their Church exhibits a deplorable failure at the intellectual level. Writer after writer concludes his essay by calling for hard thinking to be done—both theological and sociological. Raymond Plant joins the chorus of appeals for greater intellectual seriousness about the Church's involvement in society grounded in 'a developed theological understanding of man as a political animal'. The Church must equip itself to compete in the marketplace of ideas:

> We live in a world of ideologies, of visions of the good society and the good for man, which in this century have received considerable and sophisticated theoretical elaboration. Until the Church takes its task of developing a political theology in the light of its own understanding of God and . . . of human life more seriously . . . its forays into politics are going to seem as rootless and naive as its critics take them to be. (Moyser (ed.), p. 336)

In their joint chapter on the role of archbishops and bishops in politics, Medhurst and Moyser point out that there are strong constraints on Church leaders to be irenic figures, exercising a reconciling and healing ministry, promoting harmony and consensus. However, they warn that apparent harmony 'may cloak sullen acquiescence or even massive alienation perhaps having long-term destabilising consequences' (Moyser (ed.), p. 80). From this point of view it is undoubtedly healthy to have the occasional gadfly among the bishops to ask awkward questions and to bring conflicts into the open. The two authors advocate that those bishops equipped for it—and a greater division of labour is encouraged here—should engage in strategic long-term thinking about theological, moral and social questions.

This concern links up with John Macquarrie's papers 'The Bishop and the Theologian' and 'Politics as Lay Ministry'. Macquarrie has reservations about an increased role for bishops in political issues. Arguing for an essentially lay political involvement by the Church, he observes that bishops and other clerics are often politically naïve, lacking direct involvement in industry, commerce or government, and concludes: 'A few active and intelligent lay Christians involved in the political process are worth a thousand sententious utterances by bishops and synods' (Macquarrie, pp. 201f.). But the laity also have a theological role. They alone know 'the state of play in the secular world', and without their participation bishops and theologians 'may fall to discussing questions which are sadly out of touch with where people are living today' (p. 186). Ideally, Macquarrie observes, the bishop and the theologian ought to be one and the same person. Once it was so (we think of Lightfoot, Westcott, Gore, Temple and Ramsey), but today the pressures are such that it is extremely difficult to combine the two roles and we are reluctantly compelled to accept that usually the bishop and the theologian will be different men or women. Macquarrie insists, however, that bishops should possess theological minds and carry theological learning, while theologians, for their part, should 'hold themselves open and available as far as possible to the Church' (pp. 179ff.). (Macquarrie himself is of course an outstanding example of a theologian operating in the service of the Church, yet without becoming the tool of an ideology.)

Rational, calm, well-informed theological debate in the Church's synods enhances the Church's public image. The behaviour of the Church of England's General Synod compares favourably with that of the House of Commons. The leaders of the Church, bishops and archbishops, should therefore be theologically equipped to promote, enable and lead this sort of discussion. They will require a breadth of theological formation and a soundness of theological judgement for themselves and will be committed to the enterprise of theology. They will naturally want to use and acknowledge theological expertise; the Church must 'own' its theologians even when they are irritating gadflies—*especially* when they are gadflies! Affirming theologians in their work also involves defending their right to ask awkward questions.

Church leaders will therefore strive to ensure that the best theological talent—irrespective of churchmanship, up to a point—will be employed on the Church's commissions. If the quality of their work is below par they will not be afraid to say so. Thus they will be prepared to challenge the complacency and conceit to which academics are not entirely immune. At the same time, leaders will be committed to further closing the gap between academic theology and the parishes, not least by promoting the highest standards of theological education of the clergy (including post-ordination and in-service training) and by encouraging the theological development of the laity. They will show, by precept and example, that they expect the clergy to be informed, to read and to attend courses.

In a recent survey of theological training in Britain, it emerged that the great majority of centres saw the Christian minister as primarily a preacher and teacher of the faith, with these two models receiving highest priority over all. Anglican theological colleges, in particular, identified 100 per cent with the model of the minister as a learned expounder of the faith (though Anglican non-residential courses only identified with this model 67 per cent: Bunting, pp. 53, 30). This conception of the minister's role bears strongly on the professional status of the sacred ministry. As Anthony Russell has pointed out, knowledge is the basis of the authority and legitimation of a profession and this is borne out by the process of initiation—in the case of clergy, by selection, training and ordination:

> A professional body may be regarded as a separate sub-culture into which a postulant enters only after selection, training, examination and certification, culminating in a ritual which has some of the significance of a *rite de passage*. This period of initiation is characterised by instruction in a body of knowledge that has been organised into a coherent system. The initiate is required to familiarise himself with the system of abstract propositions that account in general terms for the phenomena comprising the profession's interest. This preoccupation with systematic theory is one of the principal distinguishing marks of a profession and is virtually absent in the training for non-professional roles. Knowledge is the principal resource of the professional body which is corporately concerned to develop, protect and guard it. (A. Russell, p. 11)

In the 1960s, the professional nature of the Christian ministry was under threat: clergy were unhappily confused about their role. Towler and Coxon concluded their survey of Anglican ordinands with the judgement that the similarities between the ordained ministry and other professions were 'all of form and none of content' (p. 45). They were able to make this assertion because, while they recognized that professional authority was undergirded by initiation into a body of specialized knowledge, they did not believe that the theological studies that prepared the clergy for their work deserved the status of 'knowledge'. Moreover, professionals are endowed not only with knowledge, but also with skills—and Towler and Coxon insisted that 'the clergy have no particular skills at all' (ibid.).

Writing *The Clerical Profession* in the mid-1980s, Anthony Russell was still influenced by this attitude of uncertainty and retrenchment. The clergyman's role, he believed, was no longer seen as part of the division of labour in a modern society. In a sense, it had become 'non-work':

> The clergyman does not possess skills in the sense in which the term is used in modern society, and his theological insights and pastoral experience have no market value. It is the prerequisite of an occupation that it should be able to make a definite statement about the functions and content of the role. Beyond their liturgical functions, the clergy find it particularly difficult to make statements about the content of their role in terms to which the rest of society can readily relate. (pp. 281f.)

I must confess that I find this analysis unnecessarily pessimistic for a number of reasons.

First, Towler and Coxon, in denying to theology the title of knowledge, betray a conception of what constitutes knowledge that is more than a little tinged with scientistic positivism. Of course, the chronic pluralism of Christian theology rules out any crude identification of theology and the truth of God. Theological opinion, whether sophisticated or not, professional or popular, is highly contingent and constantly changing, while the truth of God is transcendent and always eludes our faltering human grasp which can never master God. But we are not reduced to the dilemma: either mere opinion or else the absolute truth. Between the two there is *knowledge*, which, as Plato has taught us, is more than mere opinion and has to do with reality, but, as Popper has insisted, is not a synonym for truth. Knowledge is on the track of reality, homing in on a mystery that exceeds our grasp. No Christian minister could be content to accept that his or her convictions were mere opinion, and only the deluded fanatic would claim that they were identified *tout court* with God's truth. Theology is the knowledge of God and the things of God—but a critical, progressive and revisionary knowledge.

Secondly, it seems unacceptably disparaging to suggest that the clergy are lacking in professional skills. They may not possess *productive* skills, of the sort valued in an enterprise culture, but they have *facilitating* skills, like those of the teaching and caring professions. Clergy are endowed with liturgical, pastoral, inter-personal, managerial, leadership, teaching and interpretative skills. In other words, clergy have the competence to do the job.

Thirdly, I find the suggestion that these skills have no market value not a little strange, in the light of the fact that Christian congregations are willing to give regularly and generously to maintain the ordained ministry. It is not necessary that society as a whole should set a market value on such skills (and how could that be measured: by state ownership or subsidies?), provided that a significant sector of society does so. Besides, the fact that there is so little enthusiasm for disestablishment of the Church of England suggests that, in England at least, society does indeed set a value on the office and work of the clergy.

Finally, I am puzzled by the claim that the clergy are largely unable to give a coherent account of the functions and content of their role. This does not ring true to experience. Ian Bunting's recent survey of training centres reveals a sophisticated interpretation of models of the Christian ministry: as preacher and encourager of the faithful; as knowledgeable teacher and interpreter of the faith; as practical theologian who brings into a single focus the Church's thinking and practice; as priest, the representative of God and God's people; as builder and consolidator of the Christian community; as manager–facilitator of the Church's life and service; and as therapist or pastoral consultant (Bunting, pp. 28f.).

Clearly, there is an awareness of the importance of training to a high standard of professional competence. This competence comprises both knowledge and skills. A medical practitioner has both knowledge and skills: knowledge of anatomy and pathology for example. But he or she also has diagnostic skills and, hopefully, pastoral skills—the 'bedside manner'. Teachers have a knowledge of their subject and of educational philosophy, but they also have skills in communicating that knowledge in the classroom and in interpreting the academic and pastoral needs of pupils. There is an uneasy sense at the present time that the training of doctors does not adequately equip them with inter-personal skills, while the training of teachers has concentrated too heavily on classroom skills at the expense of solid academic learning that those skills are intended to enable them to deploy.

Two recent Anglican reports have argued for a reduction in the academic input of theological training courses and an increase in pastoral and interpretative skills. The report on urban deprivation *Faith in the City* (1985) called for 'a significant change in the academic requirements imposed on ordinands' in order to encourage the development of 'habits of reflection and social awareness' which would enable ministers to 'draw creatively on their resources of theology and spirituality in the face of new realities and engage in a dialogue with those of other faiths or none' (pp. 122, 119). Its rural sequel *Faith in the Countryside* (1990) endorsed this plea and argued that the pressure of academic learning in college and course syllabuses should be reduced in order to make room for instruction in collaborative ministry, management skills and 'contextual theology' (pp. 152ff.).

There is no excuse for academic theology being taught in an arid way, and it is an indictment of traditional training that many clergy give up reading and sustained theological reflection once they feel that strip of white plastic around their necks. It goes without saying that clergy need to develop 'habits of reflection and social awareness'. But it is surely not too cynical to suggest that these two recent important reports are in effect proposing that the Church of England should make the same mistake that teacher-training made in the 1960s and 1970s when it adopted a training philosophy weighted towards practical and relevant classroom skills—with its eventual pay-off: a dearth of teachers qualified to teach advanced scientific and engineering subjects. I suspect that the image that has been inadvertently fostered by this approach, of teachers as mere classroom technicians, has made no small contribution to the devaluing of the professional status of teaching as a career. Professionals are endowed with specialized learning as well as the skills to apply or communicate it.

The suggestion that the Church should cut back on academic training and increase vocational skills might seem to presuppose that the Church is groaning under the weight of a learned ministry that feels unable to cope with the pastoral demands made upon it. This is hardly our problem. Let us consider the following facts:

First, only about half of those currently being ordained into the ministry of the Church of England are graduates. While this is a slight improvement on the 40 per cent figure that was not uncommon in the 1960s, in an age of graduate professions it puts the Church's ministry at a serious disadvantage. Teaching, which is hardly the most prestigious occupation today, is now largely a graduate profession. Can the Church afford for its ordained representatives to be measured unfavourably against other groups in the teaching / caring professions?

Secondly, we live in an age of increasing specialization which the trend to all-graduate professions reflects. It is not at all uncommon for lay parishioners to be better informed theologically than their clergy, and there is an increasing demand for theological courses for lay people. The role of the minister as the learned teacher and expounder of the faith, deeply acquainted with the scriptures, is placed in jeopardy if he or she is outclassed by lay members of Bible-study and discussion groups.

Thirdly, it comes as no surprise to learn that the clergy are neglecting their studies. The Rural Church Project (vol. 2, p. 34) found that the clergy spent, on average, less than half an hour a day on study—a mere 5 per cent of their working time (and one might be forgiven for wondering what rather less than academic or theological activities this included in some cases). In his recent book on the new innovative climate in organizations, Charles Handy cites the example of a major bank insisting that 20 per cent of its managers' time be devoted to study and further training for demanding future developments. Is it unrealistic or inappropriate for the Church to demand that a minimum of a tithe of the minister's time be devoted to study and in-service training?

To sum up: the Church recognizes the need for professional competence in its ministers; that competence comprises both specialized knowledge and the skills to apply and communicate it. Traditional training was excessively weighted towards the acquisition of knowledge—the relevance of which was often lost on the young priest immersed in parish activity. There have been pressures—reinforced by two recent reports—to cut back on the academic component of training and to enlarge vocational skills. In the cultural climate that is now fast developing, that would be disastrously short-sighted. Competence is, as we have seen, the one form of authority that will gain a respectful hearing in the modern world. The Church should make training in ministerial competence, in its twofold form of learning and skills, its first priority, even if that means requiring a longer period of training from its ordinands and more rigorous and exacting forms of post-ordination and in-service training. The extra expenditure that this will necessitate should be one of the first calls on the Church's budget and should be accompanied by rigorous scrutiny of how effectively that money is spent. Jesus Christ seems to have made training for leadership and ministry one of his top priorities, keeping his disciples by his side for three intensive years.

9

The Art of Leadership

Organizations have managers, but institutions need leaders, according to Philip Selznick. Organizations exist for a utilitarian purpose, and when that purpose has been attained they become expendable. But institutions are natural communities with historical roots; they are deeply embedded in the fabric of society and have developed a legitimating ideology; they incorporate various contending interest groups and are concerned with the creation and protection of élites who are the bearers of institutional value; they are thus 'infused with value' beyond the requirements of the task in hand and are concerned with the maintenance of their own identity and resistant to change (Selznick, pp. 5–20). This is a perfect fit for the Christian churches, which permeate the fabric of society, have their roots deep in the past, are obsessed with their institutional survival and success, have their value-bearing élite in the clergy, and a legitimating ideology in their theologies. Such institutions, insists Selznick, require leadership not mere management.

How disturbing then to discover the lack of importance attached to the leadership role in the Church by clergy and those who train them. It is perhaps not too surprising to learn that in 1967 not one of nearly 100 Anglican clergy in Greater London regarded the role of organizer/administrator as the most important role for the clergy, because that does smack of mere management. It is more significant that research done ten years later found that the leadership role was near the bottom of the list, behind pastor, celebrant, preacher, counsellor, and higher only than administrator and official/representative (A. Russell, p. 276). It is most disturbing of all to discover that in a survey of theological training centres in Great Britain in 1988, the goal of 'flexible and reflective leadership' was given lowest priority, after spiritual formation, training to be a lifelong learner, laying a theoretical foundation, and equipping ordinands for practice. Anglican colleges in particular gave a very low priority to the goal of training leaders for the Church. Ian Bunting concluded that 'the low level of emphasis and support for this goal, which is carefully qualified to take into account modern theories of management, reflects an uncertainty among theological trainers about the nature of the leadership required in the churches of today' (Bunting, pp. 38ff.).

Leadership in the Christian Church is an exceedingly demanding challenge—an almost impossible role—for three reasons.

(a) THE LEADER HAS A SYMBOLIC ROLE

A leader's functions are not fully quantifiable. He or she is the bearer of an emotional investment on the part of the members of the institution, the recipient of numerous projections. This makes the leader a symbolic figure and, whatever we may go on to say about leadership, we should never lose sight of the tacit dimension of leadership and the unconscious dynamics that surround it. Selznick's emphasis on the leader as the bearer of values emphasizes this symbolic function. The institutional leader, he writes, is 'primarily an expert in the promotion and protection of values' (p. 28). The doyen of management science, Chester Barnard, in *The Functions of the Executive* (1938), called this elusive symbolic role in leadership the power to create *faith*. He spoke of

> the power of individuals to inspire cooperative personal deci-
> sion by creating faith: faith in common understanding, faith
> in the probability of success, faith in the ultimate satisfaction
> of personal motives, faith in the integrity of objective author-
> ity, faith in the superiority of common purpose as a personal
> aim of those who partake in it. (Barnard, p. 259)

Faith, for Barnard, was 'the catalyst by which the living system of human efforts is enabled to continue its incessant interchanges of energies and satisfactions'—a remarkably precocious anticipation of systems theory applied to organizations. He added that co-operation was the creative process that produced the goods, but leadership was 'the indispensable fulminator of its forces' (ibid.).

The leader's symbolic function strongly suggests that a leader must be alert to his or her role in people's fantasies. We are used to the idea that the behaviour of individuals is affected by unconscious psychological factors, but we do not reckon so readily with the truth that the behaviour of organizations is also psychologically motivated. Both individuals and groups behave in ways that are not explicable in terms of their rational and conscious intentions. These unconscious motives affect the decisions that are made: the solution of simple problems is complicated or frustrated by such unconscious forces as jealousy, guilt, anxiety and the struggle for power (cf. Rice, 1965, pp. 9f.).

The role of institutions as providing a defence against anxiety—shielding their members from reality—has been explored notably by Isabel Menzies and Elliott Jaques. Menzies showed in a celebrated study of nursing in a major hospital how the situation confronting a nurse bears a striking resemblance to the fantasies that exist at the deepest and most primitive level of every person's psyche. While this provided therapeutic opportunities for working out these tensions in contact with reality, at the same time it had an adverse effect on the quality of nursing care as defence mechanisms militated against personal involvement. Menzies drew the general conclusion that:

> The success and viability of a social institution are intimately connected with the techniques it uses to contain anxiety. . . .
> An understanding of this aspect of the functioning of a social institution is an important diagnostic and therapeutic tool in facilitating social change. (p. 39)

The resistance encountered in effecting change within an institution is a function of the institution's role in providing a dependable defence against anxiety. Thus the constructive management of change requires an analysis of anxieties held in common together with the unconscious collusions that underlie the social defences that determine our network of relationships and alliances.

Jaques himself has pointed out that change is demanded and implemented precisely when 'phantasy social relations within an institution no longer serve to reinforce individual defences against psychotic anxiety'—that is to say, anxiety in relation to the environment, to reality. Imposed changes that fail to take account of the way individuals use institutions to cope with such anxieties are likely to encounter passionate resistance (Jaques in Klein *et al.*, p. 498).

The truth of this analysis will be feelingly corroborated by Church leaders and clergy who bear the brunt of emotional reactions to such changes as new liturgies, the amalgamation of parishes, and the ordination of women priests. This is not an argument against change—that would be to collude with the unreconstructed fantasies of Church people and to evade reality—but it is a salutary warning that change must be handled in a therapeutic way; one which, above all, supports groups and individuals who feel threatened by change, during the transitional period.

There is an urgent message for such institutions as the Church in this analysis, for when an institution is being used by its members primarily as a defence against anxiety, it cannot be used to prosecute its primary task. The danger then is that the primary task may become redefined in an introverted way, concerned with the preservation of the institution for its own sake—a way that spells disaster, as we shall see, for the vitality of any organization (cf. Rice, 1963, pp. 255, 262f.).

It is, however, the leader who is particularly exposed to the risk of manipulating—and being manipulated by—the unconscious fantasies of members. Melanie Klein identified the unconscious phenomenon of *splitting*, separating in early infancy good and bad experiences of the same object (breast) or person (mother). It is a mark of maturity that one can accept that emotions of love and of hate can be felt for the same person, without resorting to the sort of dichotomous, dualistic thinking that we mentioned earlier as an impediment to dealing effectively with reality. But most of us are still prone to idealize those individuals who are in a position to affect our lives, who are experienced as loving and protective, and to denigrate those whom we encounter as antagonistic and obstructive. The dilemma of a person in a position of responsibility is that they are compelled to be occasionally obstructive to the very people whom, most of the time, they gladly support and affirm. So our difficulty in accepting that love and hate can be felt towards the same person is intensified in the case of leaders (cf. Miller and Rice, p. 16).

Bion explored the dependency syndrome that he found to be one of the ways in which small groups channelled their anxiety to avoid an encounter with reality. The leader who neither rallies his troops for combat with an external enemy (fight), nor runs away from reality (flight), but instead is committed to therapeutic work with the group, is not easily understood. In a dependent group, the leader is exalted to superhuman level: 'the feeling of security derived from the dependent group is indissolubly linked with feelings of inadequacy and frustration, and is dependent on the attribution of omnipotence and omniscience to one member—the leader' (Bion, p. 94).

In Bion's view, religion is primarily concerned with the handling of dependency and the problem of leadership is particularly acute in a community of faith. A religious group deals with leadership as though handling dynamite. It tends either to make the leader divine or to make a god the leader. In a dependent group, the members have a relationship with the leader rather than with each other (pp. 122, 130). Members of dependent groups often assume that the leader has greater powers than he or she actually has and 'develop fantasies about the destructive or magically helpful ways in which he might or might not use his power' (Whitaker, p. 375). Possibly we see this in an extreme form in the irrational belief of the Germans at the end of the Second World War, as the Russian armies fought their way into Berlin, that Hitler was about to unleash secret weapons of unprecedented destructive power that would reverse the tide of war and bring victory.

A leader must beware of colluding with the fantasies of the group. Bion warns that the leader is as much the creature of the group's operative basic assumption (such as dependence) as is any other member. The leader is likely to be someone whose personality lends itself to obliteration (Bion's word) by the basic assumption requirements of the group. The leader may become progressively detached from reality and given up to the fantasy role thrust upon him. Then the group may be led by 'an individual whose qualification for the job is that his personality has been obliterated, an automaton' (Bion, pp. 177f.). Thus strong leaders in Church or state may become the victims of their carefully cultivated reputation, moulded by the projected fantasies of thousands of their followers. Margaret Thatcher came to believe that she was invincible and neglected to cultivate her power-base. Pope John Paul II was fashioned as a spiritual leader in the adversarial ideological conflict of the Cold War period which promoted dichotomous, dualistic thinking: it is unlikely that he could lend his authority to liberal reforms even if his advisers were persuaded of their merits.

On the other hand, truly therapeutic leadership can enable individuals to come to terms with their deep anxieties. A leader who does not feed on people's dependence but helps to liberate them from it supportively is the sort of leader that every institution—and most of all, the Church—needs. Individuals will feel safe enough to take risks 'if they can hold on to the sense that there is one person in the group who retains sufficient understanding, strength, courage and disinterest to handle acutely difficult situations and emergencies should they arise' (Whitaker, p. 382). These leaders are the 'catalysts' who enable dependence to be overcome or put into proportion because they themselves enjoy comparative freedom from anxiety-based reactions to the problems of authority and possess the freedom to be creative in searching for ways to reduce tension in the group (cf. Bennis *et al.* (eds), p. 339). Therapeutic leaders who give back dependency rather than feeding on it, are what Charles Handy calls 'post-heroic' leaders. 'Whereas the heroic manager of the past knew all, could do all, and could solve every problem, the post-heroic manager asks how every problem can be solved in a way that develops other people's capacity to handle it' (1989, p. 132). This sounds to me uncannily like the way in which Jesus Christ offered leadership and exercised authority.

(b) THE LEADER FOCUSES THE ENERGIES OF THE INSTITUTION ON ITS
    PRIMARY TASK
'Leadership is the capacity to attract followers in task performance' (Reed, p. 165). The term 'primary task' was originated by A. K. Rice of the Tavistock Institute, and has passed into common management parlance. But beyond this usage lies W. R. Bion's analysis of group dynamics. Bion made a fundamental distinction between a group that was merely seeking the expression of basic psychological needs and assumptions and avoiding reality by fight/flight, pairing or dependence (the 'basic assumption group'), and the group that was motivated to work at its problems therapeutically and in the light of reality ('the work group'). The work group got on with its task, enabled by its leader or leaders (Bion, pp. 98ff.).

This primary task is described by others in terms of 'vision' or 'mission'. Handy writes that 'a leader shapes and shares a vision which gives point to the work of others' (1989, p. 106). The task-function of the leader, suggests Handy, includes initiating, information seeking, diagnosing, opinion seeking, evaluating, and decision managing (1985, p. 177). The vocabulary of vision is preferable to the once-fashionable talk of goals and objectives ('management by objectives') associated with Peter Drucker, because it suggests the unquantifiable symbolic loading of community purpose. A leader is not merely concerned with announcing pragmatic targets, but with articulating the deepest aspirations of a faith community. It is no accident that 'vision' is a term with religious and mystical overtones.

So too is 'mission', which is favoured by Selznick. The key task of leadership, he writes, is to define the institution's mission and role creatively; to relate it to internal and external factors; to embody it in the social structure of the institution so that it shapes its character (Selznick, pp. 62f.). This mission is concerned with more than mere survival: it is motivated towards success for the enterprise.

The penalty for failure to define the primary task, vision or mission of an institution—either because it serves more than one, or because it denies the one—is confusion in the organization, the blurring of its values, and inability to evaluate task performance (Rice, 1963, p. 190).

We may discern four stages of articulating and implementing this primary task or mission: vision, policy, strategy and tactics (cf. Vickers, 1973, pp. 171ff.).

(i) *Vision* is the all-embracing context for an institution's activity —the highest level of corporate consciousness. This constellation of convictions, values and absolutes answers the question 'Why?'—Why are we here? Why are we committed to our cause? Why do we believe it is important? Why should we have a programme of action at all? The level of values and norms operates in the world of ultimate imperatives, of the most basic sense of obligation, and its key word is *ought*.

(ii) *Policy*. Those ultimate values and norms give rise to policy which correlates the central vision with institutional needs and questions. While values and norms are the subject of broad consensus—after all, they are embodied chiefly in symbols, which allows for some breadth of interpretation—policies are subject to discussion and debate. In policy we move from the question 'Why?' to the question 'What?'—What do we want to do to put our basic vision into effect? Its key word is *want*. Policies are governed by what is desirable rather than what is practicable.

(iii) *Strategy*. Since policies themselves contain no practical measures to implement them, we move to the stage of strategy. Strategies are overall plans for deploying our resources in order to implement our policies most effectively. Since strategies have to take account of innumerable factors and regional variations, the scope for discussion and disagreement is that much greater. To be effective, strategies must be devolved to the regional level. An overall prescription for all contexts will be disastrous. Strategies answer the question 'How?': How best can we put our policies, based on our supreme values and norms, into effect with the maximum impact on the lives of individuals and groups? The key word in strategy is *must*: What must we do to carry out policy?

(iv) *Tactics*. Finally, strategies do not constitute the sharp end of corporate action. They are still too generalized and dominated by theory. Though partly devolved, they are not localized enough. To achieve maximum contact 'on the ground' we descend to the level of tactics. Tactics can only be handled by those on the spot. So it is vital for local staff to be party to the three higher stages: vision, policy and strategy. Since, as is well known, participants at the lower or broader levels of an institution do not respond favourably to directives and instructions handed down from on high, there is no alternative to taking them into the confidence of the policy-makers and strategists and helping them to feel that they have an essential part— rather, *the* essential part—to play in making the organization effective. By so doing we enable the vital function of *feedback* —both positive and negative—to operate in the system and acknowledge the reality that policy is made not only at the top but also by the day-to-day decisions of those who administer it. 'The task of "deciding" pervades the entire administrative organization quite as much as does the task of "doing" ' (H. Simon, 1955, p. 1). As Vickers has pointed out, the policy-maker is also dependent on all those who have the legal or practical power to veto policy, as well as that broad company whose confidence and concurrence are vital to make it effective (1965, p. 92).

Tactics, like strategy, answers the question 'How?' but on a smaller scale. Its key word is *can*: only those on the spot are in a position to know what can be done to achieve the aims set out in policy and mediated to them through strategy. In this respect, it is true once again that a chain is as strong as its weakest link.

In the Christian Church it is the task of theologians to bring to focus the central vision of Christianity and to reflect on its supreme values and norms. In performing this vital task, without which there could be no policy, and therefore no action, they attend to scripture, tradition and reason. But their task is not merely academic, for they must also be guided by the liturgies, rituals and other symbolic performances of the Church and by a sense of pastoral reality. It is a matter of simple fact that the Christian vision has taken various forms through the centuries. Though certain landmarks (dogmas) remain constant, the overall landscape has changed markedly. A number of salient features, such as the divine right of kings, the temporal power of popes, eternal punishment and the intrinsic merits of virginity have all but disappeared. Theologians will therefore not be expected simply to repeat in modern language what their predecessors in the fourth, the sixteenth or the nineteenth centuries said, but to wrestle afresh with the substance of the faith in the light of modern knowledge and contemporary concerns.

Theologians will be involved also at the level of policy-making, but only as consultants (unless they happen to be synodical representives or bishops also). Policies are formulated by the councils of the Church: synods and the college of bishops, drawing on the work of theologians, perhaps mediated through commissions which attempt to match theological insights with accurate interpretations of the contemporary world drawn from non-theological disciplines, especially the social sciences, medicine and philosophical ethics.

While policies are formulated by the Church (or churches) corporately, strategies are for those with a broad knowledge of the territory in which they have to operate—that is to say, the bishops and their diocesan synods and councils. But already at this stage they do well to involve all those who will ultimately have to translate strategy into tactics—the parish clergy and responsible lay people—in order to create a sense of common purpose, a dynamic consensus.

(c) THE LEADER IS CALLED TO BE A PROBLEM-SOLVER

The intellectual gifts required in effective leadership are highlighted when we consider the leader's role in tackling the most difficult problems encountered by the institution. Mere administrative or management ability will not suffice—brains, creativity and innovative thinking are needed. The problems faced by any organization may arise from internal pressures or may be posed by interaction with the environment. In either case, mere containment or shuffling the components will not solve them. As Kenneth Benne has written:

Problem-solving should be task (and 'reality') oriented rather than oriented to the maintenance of the prestige of some parts of the system over other parts. Growth requires optimum orientation to confronting realities and optimum release of human energies in creating and contriving effective and appropriate responses to the realities. Channelling of energy toward the maintenance of non-functional prestige systems within the systems detracts from availability of energy for creative responses. (In Bennis *et al.* (eds), pp. 231ff.)

The same point has been made in a slightly different way by Herbert Simon, who distinguishes between programmed or routine decision-making and unprogrammed or innovative decision-making. What Simon calls 'Gresham's Law of Planning' operates here: routine decisions drive out innovative decisions. Organizations should therefore make special provision for unprogrammed decision-making or problem-solving—for example, by setting up think-tanks (1960, p. 13).

Katz and Kahn make a useful distinction between *problems* and *dilemmas*. A problem can be tackled within the existing framework; current assumptions and information are adequate. A dilemma, however, cannot be solved within the existing framework and on the basis of current assumptions—it has to be reformulated and set in a fresh light (Katz and Kahn, pp. 274ff.). This insight may suggest an answer to the question as to why Church commissions, set up to deal with an intractable problem, tend to leave everything as it was before. Either the best creative theologians are not involved or, if they are, their voices are stifled by an obsession with safeguarding the prevailing consensus. Real problems—or rather dilemmas—cannot be solved without setting the problem in a new perspective by radical thinking. Though that may be disturbing to some, it is the price that has to be paid for progress in dealing with real difficulties.

It is a fallacy that problems are solved by strong, controlling leadership. As Argyris warns, problems are not solved through the sort of meetings where the chair gives firm direction, there is an inflexible agenda, personalities are avoided, and awkward customers are denied their say. (This sounds like a description of what Cabinet meetings under Margaret Thatcher were like, by all accounts.) Leaders need to be aware of tensions and frustrations, and are well advised to give them an outlet where they can do less harm than if they are bottled up under pressure until they explode. It is the sort of discussion where individuals are encouraged to be frank, and an open and experimental approach is adopted, that tackles problems constructively. An organization that fosters conformity and detachment, with its corollaries of resentment and distrust, will go into a spiral of decline—a closed system. But one that fosters individual initiative, commitment to its cause, and frank speaking on the premise that mistakes can be forgiven and lessons learned on the basis of trust, will be effective and fruitful—an open system. Put another way, the aim must be to decrease defensive activities that absorb energy and lead to entropy, and increase the opportunities for individuals to put their energy into positive effort, bringing a sense of achievement and boosting self-esteem—the spiral of success (cf. Argyris, pp. 136ff.).

Katz and Kahn indicate a number of psychological factors that hamper effective decision-making in an organization.

First, there is *social determination*, the influence of the environment. Any successful system functions through interchange with its environment and this interchange is monitored through boundary control. It does not mean capitulating to the environment but participating in a fruitful exchange. This suggests that, while the Church cannot close its borders to the surrounding society—that would spell death to any living system; it must be prepared to respond constructively to stimuli—it must not allow itself to be swamped.

Secondly, *identification* with outside groups, especially emotional ties with groups of superior status. 'Many poor organizational decisions are made on the basis of overweighty information from powerful and illustrious sources irrelevant to the problem' (Katz and Kahn, p. 286). Does this not well describe the feelings of a small Christian communion seeking its own authentic way ahead, but tempted to be continually looking over its shoulder to more prestigious Christian communions with a stronger grasp of authority?

The converse of identification is *projection*, where we project our own attitudes and emotions on to the other party and imagine them as thinking like us. If we are disposed to be magnanimous towards the other side, it might be a rash miscalculation to assume that this generosity will be reciprocated. One the other hand, if we are engaged in rather Machiavellian tactics to gain our ends, we are likely to impute similar sinister plotting to the opposition—perhaps unjustly.

Two further forms of inadequate approaches to problem-solving are *global* or undifferentiated thinking, which treats all problems and situations in the same way, and *dualistic* or dichotomized thinking, which sees everything in simplistic, black and white terms.

Attention to the particular in its individual context, rather than immediately invoking precedent, or splitting the parties into 'us' and 'them', for and against, is the constructive way to approach a problem.

The final psychological handicap is what Katz and Kahn call 'cognitive myopia': shortsightedness, responding only to the immediate, the visible, the palpable, rather than searching for deeper, long-term causes and attempting to deal with them. Any institution that lives from hand to mouth in this way will soon be overtaken by those deep, long-term trends. As Antony Jay has put it: other people can cope with the waves; it is the leader's job to watch the tide (Jay, p. 139). To sum up the problem-solving role of the leader, let me quote Jay's remark: 'You can judge a leader by the size of problem he tackles—people nearly always pick a problem their own size' (ibid.).

10

Harnessing Conflict

A war of all against all was how Thomas Hobbes described the natural state of humanity (*De Cive*, pp. 117f.). The state of nature was a condition of 'absolute liberty', equivalent to anarchy. 'Without a common power to keep them all in awe, they are in that condition which is called war; and such a war as is of every man, against every man' (*Leviathan*, p. 143). The antidote to absolute liberty was absolute authority—Leviathan. The group therapist W. R. Bion is echoing Hobbes when he claims that 'the individual is a group animal at war, both with the group and with those aspects of his personality that constitute his "groupishness" ' (p. 168). Conflict is endemic within a community as well as where no real community exists.

Furthermore, authority does not suppress conflict but promotes it. Authority is the capacity to effect change in the society and in the lives of individuals. So the exercise of power necessarily generates conflict. Conflict and power feed on one another. The more prevalent conflict in a society becomes, the more power will be valued and the more individuals will hunger for it as giving them the ability to protect and promote their interests and those of their dependants (cf. Kahn in Kahn and Boulding (eds), pp. 1-3). This can set up a spiral of decline into Hobbes's vicious natural state of humanity.

MacIntyre has reminded us that in a flourishing society conflict remains in the form of argument and disagreement about the aims of that society. A tradition is always partly constituted by an ongoing argument about those 'goods' whose pursuit gives the tradition its *raison d'être*. 'Traditions, when vital, embody continuities

119

of conflict. . . . A living tradition, then, is an historically extended, socially embodied argument, and argument precisely in part about the goods which constitute that tradition' (MacIntyre, pp. 206f.). This insight has been developed in reference to the Christian Church in the writings of Stephen Sykes on authority and the essence of Christianity—the essence of Christianity being 'the goods' in MacIntyre's terms (Sykes, 1984).

Conflict is not only inescapable, but indispensable. The deleterious effects of unrestrained conflict are obvious. It reduces collaboration between various components or sub-groups of the organization. It leaves the defeated damaged and unfit for productive work. It wastefully diverts energy from work to warfare. It polarizes conflicting groups or individuals in a way that may take years to overcome. On the other hand, conflict gives vitality to an institution. It allows internal interest groups to pursue their aims, which may be for the overall benefit of the system. It opens up the system to its environment as fresh energies are drawn in to replace those energies consumed in internal conflicts. It clarifies the true interests of the organization, corrects imbalances, and stimulates reform and renewal (cf. Sofer, p. 223; Selznick, pp. 94, 368). All attempts to create a 'totally homogeneous, unargumentative, non-disputatious' organization, have tended, as Charles Handy insists, to result in low output and low morale (1985, p. 255).

'Conflict is endemic in human affairs', states Geoffrey Vickers, 'and its management is the most characteristically human function and skill' (1973, p. 153). If conflict is not only inevitable but also indispensable, the aim must be to harness it for the good of the organization, and to channel it into constructive argument and competitive standards of attainment. Selznick asserts that it is the task of leadership, in embodying the purpose of the organization, 'to fit the aims of the organization to the spontaneous interests of the groups within it, and conversely, to bind parochial group egotism to larger loyalties and aspirations' (p. 93).

The role of leadership in conflict is not the same as the role of management. The job of a manager is to contain conflict, to mediate and to reconcile. But the leader's calling is to harness conflict to serve the overall mission of the institution. Since conflict is inevitable, it should not be allowed to exhaust its participants and to paralyse the institution, but should be channelled away from infighting to confront challenges emerging from the environment. Putting it crudely: as far as the Church is concerned, evangelicals should be urged to evangelize with all their might, catholics should be encouraged to offer worship in the beauty of holiness, and liberals should be confirmed in their social concern—to keep them all from one another's throats! Where the natural outlet is thwarted, energies become turned inwards and become self-destructive. Since the activities of evangelism, worship and social action belong to the primary task of the Church, some division of labour is appropriate. Where there is mutual learning on the basis of mutual unconditional acceptance in the framework of communion—*koinonia* (Avis, 1990)—evangelicals, catholics and liberals will take on board one another's ultimate concerns, resulting in healthy cross-fertilization rather than autonomous activity in sterile isolation.

I now offer a number of guidelines that should assist the delicate task of harnessing conflict.

(a) ACT POSITIVELY AND AVOID PROVOCATION

Constructive action enjoys a presumption in its favour. It carries conviction with those on the receiving end, enhances the corporate sense of purpose and—provided it is consistent—generates momentum within the organization. Where negative actions—such as cuts in expenditure, abolition of posts, reductions in activity, disciplinary measures—are required, they should be incorporated, as far as possible, in an overall programme of positive action. In other words, defective activity should be replaced with something better.

Initiatives and programmes should be carefully costed, in human and financial terms, both for obvious budgetary reasons and in order to deprive critics of a ready handle for attack. Those responsible must be satisfied that the beneficial results that are anticipated (the 'pay-off') exceed the cost of the programme. The Archbishops' Commission on Rural Areas (ACORA) in its report *Faith in the Countryside* made an estimated 150 concrete recommendations of which only two (clergy stipend increases and honoraria for clergy wives) were costed out—and those apparently inaccurately.

The converse of positive action is avoiding provocation. Leaders may in theory have the authority to issue binding directives, but if these are greeted with mere grudging acquiescence it will be counter-productive. Acquiescence is incompatible with a climate of trust and willing effort. Classic management studies demonstrated that autocracy produced a negative response and that democratic,

121

consultative and persuasive methods were the most fruitful. Participants are only motivated to co-operate if they have been involved in the process of decision-making. That investment of mental energy 'cathects' (as Freudians would say) the decision for them (de Board, p. 140).

A provocative incident can be the catalyst for an explosion of unanticipated conflict. It can bring to a head stored up but hitherto unfocused resentments and fears. The Bishop of Durham, Dr David Jenkins, is an example of a leader who has not exactly gone out of his way to avoid being provocative, and who has consequently reaped a harvest of hostility from traditionalists (no doubt more than compensated for by the gratitude of doubters, seekers and half-believers). It does not follow that Church leaders can never speak their minds frankly or handle controversial issues, but it does suggest the wisdom of consolidating one's power-base first by becoming known, trusted and (please God) loved. Even sensitive issues can be handled in a non-provocative way that does not polarize opinion and offer an outlet for all sorts of irrelevant and extraneous projections.

(b) COMMUNICATE PERSUASIVELY

The opposite of persuasive communication was described by Tom Burns as a system where information goes up through a system of filters and commands and prohibitions come down through a series of loudspeakers (cited Jay, p. 80). The further an organization can move away from that model towards the sensitive reception of information and feedback from the roots of the organization and towards leadership by example, encouragement and incentives, the more healthy and productive that organization will be. Effective communication, in the sense of the exchange of information and the transmission of meaning and purpose, is the very essence of a successful organization, just as damaging forms of communication are at the heart of a failed organization (cf. Katz and Kahn, p. 223). Chester Barnard regarded communication as a virtual synonym for authority. Herbert Simon gives his opinion that no stage of the administrative process 'is more generally ignored or more poorly performed' than communicating decisions. Communication has failed, he points out, whenever it is forgotten that the behaviour of individuals is the instrument through which the organization achieves its purposes (H. Simon, 1955, p. 108).

Management wisdom insists that communication needs to be

selective, concise and undistorted; conveyed through people rather than through procedures; passed through the shortest and most direct channels available; and received as appreciative, supportive and persuasive.

There is a therapeutic dimension to communication. In Bion's scheme, communication is a function of the 'work' group—the therapeutic community. But the more the group corresponds to the 'basic assumption' group—motivated to defence and evading reality—'the less it makes any rational use of verbal communication' (Bion, p. 185). Foulkes endorses this insight, insisting that a group can only grow through what it can share; it can only share what it can communicate; and it can only communicate through what it already has in common—that is to say, language (Foulkes, p. 31). If the Church is to be a truly therapeutic community, where human beings are being made whole, through a deepening knowledge of one another and of themselves on the basis of unconditional mutual acceptance (Avis, 1989b, ch. 10), priority must be given to wholesome communication. The Christian Church is certainly not exempt from the psychopathological symptoms and therapeutic dynamics invoked by group therapy. Indeed, if Bion is to be believed, the Church is a paradigm case of a group motivated by dependence and fighting shy of reality. Foulkes's words are therefore applicable to the Christian community:

> It is in the process of communication and the struggle for it that all the other dynamics meet . . . neurotic disturbances, symptoms in themselves autistic and unsuitable for sharing, exert for this very reason an increasing pressure upon the individual for expressing them. . . . Working towards an ever more articulate form of communication is . . . identical with the therapeutic process itself. (Foulkes, p. 169)

What authority do the Church's leaders have, in the final analysis? Is it not a moral and pastoral authority, exercised through persuasion, encouragement, example, support and guidance? Working in a community of freely given loyalty and service, the clergy certainly do not command obedience or expect unquestioning submission. Our idea of authority in the Church would seem to be moving closer to the way that Jesus himself dealt with individuals and situations: by appealing to an individual's better nature, by holding out acceptance and forgiveness, by offering the unconditional love and support that enables people to find the answer within themselves.

It is perhaps relevant to the current debate over the role of women in the Church's ministry to observe that many women actually exercise this kind of authority better than most men. Kathleen Jones has asked whether the exclusion of the feminine from the practice of authority in a patriarchal culture has contributed to the tendency to identify authority with rationalized compulsion. Referring to the work of Carol Gilligan, she comments that 'what constitutes authority for women is exactly what is most feared by men: sustained connections'. Jones proposes an ideal of 'compassionate authority', adding that compassion has the potential to humanize authority (Pennock and Chapman (eds), pp. 156, 159, 165).

A glance at the nature of authority in other spheres of modern Western life—marriage, the family, teaching, therapy, the role of the specialist or consultant in general—confirms the changes that the notion of authority has undergone and the personal, moral character of authority as understood today. In place of unquestioned, reified authority, which must be obeyed because of what it is in itself, we find an appeal to discussion, respect, example and consensus. This is a matter of simple perception and it supports the contention of the Jungian therapist H. Dieckmann that we need to understand authority 'not as a static, unchanging innate principle, granted to man by the will of God, but as a principle capable of changing, of taking different forms of growth and of development towards certain goals which are, in the final analysis, determined by our value systems' (Dieckmann, p. 233).

The gospels portray a Jesus who taught with authority (Mark 1.22), healed with authority (Mark 1.27), claimed the allegiance of his disciples with authority ('Follow me!') and absolved the sins of men and women with authority (Mark 2.10). But unlike the churches that have claimed to speak in his name, Jesus skilfully avoided laying down the law both about what people were to believe (in the sense of doctrines) and about how they were to conduct themselves (rules of behaviour). If his authority was not that of a legislator, was it the authority of a charismatic personality who wins people to his side by personal magnetism? We have already discussed the ambivalent sense in which Jesus fits the description 'charismatic', but if his authority lay in the power of his personality, he could have no authority for us today. For his inner life and psychological make-up are, as is widely acknowledged in the study of the gospels, hidden from us. We have no access to the personality of Jesus Christ.

It is not his personality that we should look at for the source of his authority, but instead his character. In this sense I am happy to adopt the suggestion made in the writings of Stephen Sykes: that the character of Christ belongs to the very essence of Christianity. I take it that the 'character' of Jesus Christ is meant, not in the Aristotelian sense of the complex of dispositions, habits and personal discipline that form an individual's moral character (for that too is concealed from us in the case of Jesus), but in the sense of character as when we speak of a person of good character or of a character reference—the moral impression that Jesus Christ made on those who encountered him in his earthly ministry, from the time of his baptism by John to his 'reign' from the cross and his resurrection appearances to the disciples—and the impression that he still makes on as us we encounter him in the preaching of the gospel in the Christian Church today.

His character was and is the character of justice, goodness and love—unlimited, unalloyed, unwavering. With the eyes of faith the disciples of Jesus, then and now, see these qualities as transcendent justice, transcendent goodness and transcendent love—open to God, flowing from God, not reducible to purely human qualities. Through his moral character, Jesus mediated the reality of God. As Schleier-macher says, he intensified the consciousness of God and drew others into the power of his own God-consciousness. Through a life totally open to God and wholly at God's disposal, a life in which God was incarnate, his authority was the authority of God. It reveals the authority of God to be in no way oppressive, inhibiting, external, alienating, heteronomous, but rather liberating, enabling, personal, sustaining and creative. That is the model for the authority of the Church. Through its pastoral, sacramental 'therapy' it ought to be able to change the inherited psychic structure of humanity, that tends to sado-masochistic operations of authority, in order to re-create human nature in the Church, as the community of the body of Christ, in his image.

This Christlike method of persuasive, enabling communication can be identified in Paul's dealings with his churches. As Young and Ford have shown in their studies of 2 Corinthians, far from pulling rank with his wayward congregations, or manipulating them emotionally as Shaw maintains, Paul gives them a dignity and an independence that requires him to persuade and convince rather than merely to issue orders (though Paul is rather less subtle, persuasive and oblique in 1 Corinthians where he tackles the problems of the

Corinthian church with both fists flying!). However, as far as the second epistle is concerned, it is true to say that 'if taken at face value, the most striking feature of his language is that it is persuasive, appealing, encouraging, pleading . . . the only way Paul can have any effective authority is if the Corinthians recognise it voluntarily, from the heart. . . . His relationship with them is part of a more fundamental joint relationship with God' (Young and Ford, p. 109).

To be identified with the Christian gospel, Young and Ford conclude, is to remain in union with the one who was poor, humble, weak and dead. This entails a critique of other forms of power, authority and effectiveness. Authority therefore 'can and even must go together with what seems its denial: a slave-like existence, humiliation, vulnerability and the need to plead and persuade at every point' (pp. 210f.). This is in keeping with the very character of God as revealed in the New Testament. As Sykes has put it: 'God, the single divine source of all authority, takes the pathway among humanity of challengeability and service' (Jeffery (ed.), p. 11). It might truly be said that the act of God in Jesus Christ is an act of persuasive communication.

(c) MAXIMIZE INVOLVEMENT BUT PRESERVE DISTANCE

If those at the sharp end of the institution's efforts (in the Church, the clergy) are to be effective agents in translating strategy (determined by policy) into tactics at the local level, all human resources must be mobilized. This means maximizing the involvement of the organization's staff in policy-making and decision-taking processes. Although this is time-consuming and requires great patience and inter-personal skills, in the long run it makes for the most cost-effective and efficient use of the organization's resources because it minimizes conflict, the dispersal of energy that should be concentrated on the primary task, and the tendency of members to work at cross purposes with one another. This maximization of involvement is achieved by consultation, delegation and feedback mechanisms. The purpose is to intensify consciousness of a common set of goals. 'The general strategy is to arouse and maintain expectations of effectively shared values' (Lasswell, 1949, p. 188). The larger the number of members who are actively involved, the more responsibility for the organization and its work is shared out and the larger the pool of talent and experience that it can call upon.

A particular application of the principle of maximizing involvement is *openness to criticism*. If, as Acton said, all power tends to corrupt, one of the first facets of power to be corrupted is the ability to think objectively. Leaders, and especially those who have been leaders for some time, become insulated from critical analysis of their actions. Small groups of advisers, as Janis showed in his book *Victims of Groupthink*, tend to offer the advice they think will please. The innate drive to consensus in such an intimate group inhibits critical perspectives on problems. It is part of a therapeutic understanding of leadership that it should not stand on its prerogatives, but should invite criticism. Surely the Church, of all institutions, should be able to do this. It stands under the judgement of a transcendent God. The prophetic denunciations of idolatry constantly ring in its ears. Its 'Protestant principle' (Tillich) continually relativizes all earthly structures. A therapeutic understanding of authority that is open to enlightenment and critique is the clearest acknowledgement of the finite, sinful status of the Church. Like its master, the Church must continually negate the authority that belongs to this world, though it constantly accrues to it. It must relinquish every form of compulsion, manipulation, coercion, threat; and offer up its authority as a sacrifice that it might receive it again through God transfigured. It must penitently acknowledge its mortality, finitude and imperfection. 'An authority which has come to terms with its own extinction finds a certain security in such realism. . . . Authority which has recognised its own temporary nature need not repress criticism but can listen to it. The recognition of its own mortality is the final act of self-criticism' (Shaw, p. 20).

The converse of maximizing involvement is *preserving distance*. There is an optimum level of contact between a leader and his or her members. The span of distance that is required is that which is sufficient to safeguard the reputation of the leader as leader. There are advantages in distanced leadership. As Sofer has pointed out, where a person is confronted with two levels of authority, affection and trust tend to be directed at the higher, more distant level, while negative feelings are directed at the nearer level as the source of any feelings of deprivation, though the real cause may emanate from the top (Sofer, pp. 187f.). The regimental sergeant-major, the ship's first officer and the archdeacon are the ones who tend to bear the brunt of any dissatisfaction.

But the need to maintain distance and preserve reputation are balanced by the need to make one's presence felt. As Lasswell and Kaplan have written (quoting Michel):

> Weight of authority varies with the prestige of the authority. . . . Now prestige diminishes with increasing contact with those outside the select. . . . It follows that 'authority can neither arise nor be preserved without the establishment and maintenance of distance between those who command and those who obey'. Thus authority is characteristically accompanied by pomp and ceremony. (Lasswell and Kaplan, pp. 135f.)

This is a telling argument against proposals (such as those of the report *Faith in the Countryside*) to multiply bishops, especially suffragan bishops. The quantity of episcopal authority is probably finite: the smaller you divide it up—especially among bishops who have no real powers of jurisdiction—the more you dilute it and render it ineffective. When Newman, in the first of the *Tracts for the Times*, called upon the bishops to assert themselves, he urged them 'Magnify your office', not 'Multiply your officers'.

However, authority cannot hold itself so far aloof from its sphere of responsibility that it places a strain on its very identity. In the parable, the servant said to himself, 'My master is a long time returning' and he began to misbehave (Matthew 24.48f.). Machiavelli advised the Prince to reside in newly acquired territories. Authority must find ways to effect 'action at a distance'—telekinesis—through representatives who have its commission (archdeacons? though not as surrogate bishops) and by symbolic presence (the bishop's chair in every church?). Whitaker warns, in the context of group therapy, against too readily giving away power. Once given away, power is hard to take back again without undermining the integrity of those to whom it has been entrusted, and thus implying the message, 'I thought that I could trust you to make sensible decisions . . .'. The leader who has ultimate responsibility should retain ultimate authority (Whitaker, pp. 374f.). Just as a parish priest will be involved in every activity of the parish without carrying them out him- or herself, so Church leaders will make their presence felt without keeping a finger in every pie.

(d) GIVE APPRECIATION FOR PARTICIPATION AND
REWARD EXCEPTIONAL CONTRIBUTIONS

Since the leaders of a voluntary body like the Church enjoy a largely moral authority, they cannot afford to take anyone's contribution for granted. Clear-sighted management aims must be complemented—and perhaps cushioned—by rewards for participation. A recent study of voluntary organizations in Britain has shown that the current emphasis on importing management techniques into voluntary bodies, such as charities, is producing friction with the highly motivated work force of volunteers and the vocationally motivated employed staff who expect a say in how the organization is run. The clash between professional management techniques and the tacit rewards demanded by self-motivated staff 'may result in a fundamental redefinition of the core values and ideology of the organisation' (Butler and Wilson, p. 172; cf. pp. 163f.). Applying this to the Church, one might say that the new management awareness must not be allowed to hamper pursuit of the primary task.

Leaders of voluntary organizations must, therefore, be generous in appreciation, rewarding every participant—not merely those who have excelled in devotion to the cause—with respect and gratitude. As the parish clergy know, appreciation is half the battle: you thank people whether or not they really deserve it; you tell them how hard they have worked, even if some have been slack. This raises the standard of expectation for the next time and conveys esteem, which is the highest reward of all. Of course, verbal appreciation and esteem must be borne out by the way that affairs are actually conducted: if aspects of the administration of the institution are insensitive or demeaning, no amount of praise can compensate for the injuries so inflicted.

For employees of the organization, some rewards need to be tangible. Mere egalitarianism does not promote efficiency. By rewarding responsibility and effort, you designate those individuals as models for others to emulate. Now the clergy are highly self-motivated, so any rewards must be designed to strengthen that inner motivation that comes from a sense of vocation and the consciousness of their commission. Research suggests that in the early months of a job, the significance of the task and the feedback received on performance are the chief sources of satisfaction. After this 'honeymoon period', the variety of skills required, being one's own master (or mistress), and having a clearly defined task with a beginning and

129

an end become just as important. But after five years none of these aspects makes much difference to the satisfaction felt. It is then that contractual factors, such as pay, benefits and other conditions of service, begin to matter more (Handy, 1985, p. 31). Self-motivation does need reinforcing by such mundane factors as remuneration and privileges, even in the Church.

Herzberg distinguished between *hygiene* factors and *motivating* factors. Hygiene factors included salary, status and working conditions. Motivating factors included a sense of achievement, recognition, responsibility and advancement (cf. Adair, p. 132). This is a somewhat misleading dichotomy. It is clear that salary and other privileges are indicators of achievement and recognition, which, as Maslow showed, top the hierarchy of human needs, together with a sense of belonging and being loved. Gradations—carrying the possibility of promotion—convey esteem. But they only do so when they are recognized tangibly in the form of pay differentials. In his study of bureaucracy, Jaques argues that grading 'helps to define a person's public identity and may be in accord with or in conflict with his sense of private identity. It establishes the boundaries of his current potential reward. It is a means of comparing the level of his role and that of others. It sets a major framework within which he formulates and pitches his immediate level of aspiration' (Jaques, p. 277). Advancement—or the possibility of advancement—is needed in an organization because it confers status and so increases influence (power); it compensates for the burden of responsibility and the accompanying stresses; it provides evidence of personal effectiveness and confirms that one is channelling one's efforts in the right direction (cf. Sofer, p. 229).

Promotions to senior positions are the most potent way in which an institution signals to its own membership and to an audience that transcends its membership, what its scale of values and priority aims are. Jay writes:

> You can issue directives and policy statements and messages to staff until the waste paper baskets burst, but they are nothing compared with promotions. Promotions are the one visible, unmistakable sign of a corporation's standard of values, an irrevocable declaration of the qualities it prizes in its staff, a simultaneous warning and example to everyone who knows the nature of the job and the qualities of its new incumbent. (Jay, pp. 169f.)

Jay adds that Gresham's Law—that bad currency drives out good—operates more swiftly and inexorably through promotions than through any other agency (ibid.).

Let us now ask why differentials are desirable in the Church.

(i) Differentials encourage reasonable mobility among the clergy by providing a basic career structure. This helps to minimize stagnation and frustration. Frustration leads to regression in mental attitude and to unco-operative and destructive behaviour.

(ii) Differentials demonstrate that the Church places a value on leadership qualities and managerial skills. They create a climate in which clergy will learn to ask: 'What needs in the Church are not being met? What qualities does the Church think are important besides prayerfulness and faithfulness? How can I best prepare myself in my present post for a bigger challenge in the next?'

(iii) Differentials give incentives to cope with added burdens and stress. These may take the form of greater responsibilities in terms of population, plant or personnel; heavier work load as individuals voluntarily take on tasks beyond the immediate call of duty; a stressful environment for the minister and his or her family (e.g. the inner city).

(iv) Differentials help a diocese to attract clergy of above-average ability to fill demanding posts. They send a clear message that a diocese sets great store by the gifts required to make a success of these jobs. This is already the practice in the Church of England with regard to residentiary canons, archdeacons, suffragan bishops, deans and provosts, diocesan bishops and archbishops. There is a pastoral rationale for differentials, but the bottom line is that if you don't put money into it, no one will take you seriously!

Finally, rewarding participation means passing up credit for success. Good leaders prepare the ground for what they want to do (having already ascertained by consultation that they have a mandate for it) and sow the seed which germinates in the minds of the members. Great is the leader's gratification when the members come and ask for what is already in the leader's mind! But leaders must keep their pleasure to themselves. The words of Lao Tzu are well known:

A leader is best when people barely know that he exists. Not so good when people obey and acclaim him. Much worse when they despise him. Fail to honour people and they fail to honour you. Of a good leader, who talks little, when his work is done, his aim fulfilled, they will all say, 'We did this ourselves'.

Bibliography

ABBOTT, W.M. (ed.) (1966) *The Documents of Vatican II*, London and Dublin: Geoffrey Chapman/New York: The America Press.

ADAIR, J. (1983) *Effective Leadership*, Aldershot and Brookfield, VT: Gower.

ADORNO, T.W. *et al.* (1950) *The Authoritarian Personality*, New York: Harper & Row.

Advisory Council for the Church's Ministry (1983) 'Selection for Ministry: A Report on Criteria' (ACCM Occasional Paper 12, revised 1990).

Advisory Council for the Church's Ministry (1987) 'Education for the Church's Ministry' (ACCM Occasional Paper 22).

Advisory Council for the Church's Ministry (1990) 'Ordination and the Church's Ministry: A Theological Evaluation'.

APULEIUS (1950) *The Golden Ass*, trans. R. Graves, Harmondsworth: Penguin/Cambridge, MA: Harvard University Press (Loeb Classical Library no. 44).

ARATO, A. and GEBHARDT, E. (eds) (1978) *The Essential Frankfurt School Reader*, Oxford: Blackwell/New York: Urizen.

ARCHER, A. (1986) *The Two Catholic Churches*, London: SCM.

ARENDT, H. (1977) 'What is Authority?' in *Between Past and Future*, Harmondsworth and New York: Penguin.

ARGYRIS, C. (1964) *Integrating the Individual and the Organization*, New York: Wiley.

AVIS, P.D.L. (1986a) *Foundations of Modern Historical Thought: From Machiavelli to Vico*, Beckenham, Kent: Croom Helm/New York: Methuen.

133

AVIS, P.D.L. (1986b) *Methods of Modern Theology*, Basingstoke: Marshall Pickering.

AVIS, P.D.L. (1989a) *Anglicanism and the Christian Church*, Edinburgh: T. & T. Clark/Minneapolis: Augsburg/Fortress Press.

AVIS, P.D.L. (1989b) *Eros and the Sacred*, London: SPCK/Wilton, CT: Morehouse.

AVIS, P.D.L. (1990) *Christians in Communion*, London: Geoffrey Chapman Mowbray/Collegeville, MN: Liturgical Press.

BARNARD, C. (1938) *The Functions of the Executive*, Cambridge, MA: Harvard University Press.

BARR, J. (1977) *Fundamentalism*, London: SCM/Philadelphia: Trinity Press International.

BARRETT, C.K. (1966) *The Holy Spirit and the Gospel Tradition*, 2nd edn, London: SPCK.

BARRETT, C.K. (1973) *The Second Epistle to the Corinthians*, London: Black/New York: Harper & Row.

BENNIS, W.G., BENNE, K.D. and CHIN, R. (eds) (1961) *The Planning of Change*, New York: Holt, Rinehart & Winston.

BERGSON, H. (1935) *The Two Sources of Morality and Religion*, New York: Doubleday Anchor.

BERLIN, I. (1969) *Four Essays on Liberty*, Oxford and New York: Oxford University Press.

BHASKAR, R. (1978) *A Realist Theory of Science*, Brighton: Harvester/Atlantic Highlands, NJ: Humanities Press (1975).

BILLIG, M. (1982) *Ideology and Social Psychology*, Oxford: Blackwell.

BION, W.R. (1961) *Experiences in Groups and Other Papers*, London: Tavistock.

BOFF, L. (1985) *Church, Charism and Power*, New York: Crossroad.

BRINKMAN, B.R. (1988) *To the Lengths of God*, London: Sheed.

BUNTING, I. (1990) *The Places to Train: A Survey of Theological Training in Britain*, London: Kingham Hill Trust and MARC Europe.

BUTLER, R.J. and WILSON, D.C. (1990) *Managing Voluntary and Non-Profit Organisations*, London: Routledge.

CAILLOIS, R. (1980) *Man and the Sacred*, Westport, CT: Greenwood (Glencoe, IL: Free Press, 1959).

CALVIN, J. (n.d.) *Institutes of the Christian Religion*, trans. H. Beveridge, London: Clarke/Grand Rapids, MI: Eerdmans.

CAPLAN, L. (ed.) (1987) *Studies in Religious Fundamentalism*, Basingstoke: Macmillan/Albany, NY: State University of New York Press.

DE BOARD, R. (1978) *The Psychoanalysis of Organisations*, London: Tavistock/New York: Methuen.

DIECKMANN, H. (1977) 'Some Aspects of the Development of Authority', *Journal of Analytical Psychology*, 22, pp. 230–42.

DOSTOYEVSKY, F. (1958) *The Brothers Karamazov*, trans. D. Magarshack, 2 vols, Harmondsworth and New York: Penguin.

DUGGAN, M. (1983) *Runcie: The Making of an Archbishop*, London: Hodder.

DUNCAN, H.D. (1969) *Symbols and Social Theory*, New York: Oxford University Press.

DUNN, J.D.G. (1975) *Jesus and the Spirit*, London: SCM/Philadelphia: Westminster Press.

EDWARDS, D.L. (ed.) (1990) *Robert Runcie: A Portrait by his Friends*, London: Fount.

EISENSTADT, S.N. (1968) *Max Weber: On Charisma and Institution Building*, Chicago: University of Chicago Press.

EMMET, D. (1966) *Rules, Roles and Relations*, London: Macmillan/New York: St Martin's Press.

EMMET, D. (1972) *Function, Purpose and Powers*, 2nd edn, London: Macmillan.

EVANS, C.F. (1968) *The Beginning of the Gospel*, London: SPCK.

Faith in the City: The Report of the Archbishop of Canterbury's Commission on Urban Priority Areas (1985) London: Church House.

Faith in the Countryside: The Report of the Archbishops' Commission on Rural Areas (1990) Worthing: Churchman.

FESTINGER, L. (1957) *A Theory of Cognitive Dissonance*, Stanford CA: Stanford University Press.

FEYERABEND, P. (1975) *Against Method*, London: New Left Books.

FOULKES, S.H. (1983) *Introduction to Group-Analytic Psychotherapy*, London: Maresfield (Heinemann, 1948).

FREUD, S. (1985) *Pelican Freud Library*, vol. XII, Harmondsworth and New York: Penguin.

FRIEDRICH, C.J. (ed.) (1958) *Authority* (*Nomos* I), Cambridge, MA: Harvard University Press.

FROMM, E. (1942) *The Fear of Freedom*, London: Routledge & Kegan Paul.

FROMM, E. (1982) *Greatness and Limitations of Freud's Thought*, London: Abacus/New York: NAL.

GADAMER, H.-G. (1970) *Truth and Method*, London: Sheed (2nd German edn)/New York: Crossroad.

GILBERT, M. (1988) *'Never Despair': Winston S. Churchill 1945–1965*, London: Heinemann.

GILL, R. (1989) *Competing Convictions*, London: SCM.

GILLIGAN, C. (1982) *In a Different Voice: Psychological Theory and Women's Development*, Cambridge, MA: Harvard University Press.

GOGOL, N. (1961) *Dead Souls*, trans. D. Magarshack, Harmondsworth and New York: Penguin.

GOLDINGAY, J. (ed.) (1989) *Signs, Wonders and Healing*, Leicester: IVP.

GRANT, R.M. (1952) *Miracle and Natural Law in Graeco-Roman and Early Christian Thought*, Amsterdam: North-Holland.

GUNSTONE, J. (1989) *The Wimber Phenomenon*, London: Darton, Longman & Todd.

HABGOOD, J. (1983) *Church and Nation in a Secular Age*, London: Darton, Longman & Todd.

HANDY, C. (1985) *Understanding Organisations*, 3rd edn, Harmondsworth and New York: Penguin.

HANDY, C. (1989) *The Age of Unreason*, London: Business Books.

HILL, E. (1988) *Ministry and Authority in the Catholic Church*, London: Geoffrey Chapman/Oak Park, IL: Meyer-Stone.

HOBBES, T. (1962) *Leviathan*, London: Fontana/New York: Macmillan.

HOBBES, T. (1972) *De Cive*, in *Man and Citizen*, ed. B. Gert, Brighton: Harvester.

HOGAN, R.M. and LE VOIR, J.M. (1988) *Faith for Today: The Teachings of Pope John Paul II*, London: Collins (1989)/New York: Doubleday.

HOLLOWAY, R. (1985) *The Sidelong Glance*, London: Darton, Longman & Todd.

HOLMBERG, B. (1978) *Paul and Power*, Lund: Gleerup/ Philadelphia: Fortress.

HORKHEIMER, M. (1941) 'The End of Reason', *Zeitschrift für Sozialforschung*, 9, pp. 366–88.

HORKHEIMER, M. (1972) *Critical Theory: Selected Essays*, New York: Seabury Press.

HORKHEIMER, M. and ADORNO, T.W. (eds) (1973) *Aspects of Sociology: By the Frankfurt Institute for Social Research*, London: Heinemann (1956).

HUME, B. (1988) *Towards a Civilization of Love*, London: Hodder.

JACOBS, M. (1989) *Holding in Trust: The Appraisal of Ministry*, London: SPCK.

JANIS, I.L. (1972) *Victims of Groupthink*, Boston: Houghton Mifflin.

JAQUES, E. (1976) *A General Theory of Bureaucracy*, London: Heinemann/New York: Halsted.

JAY, A. (1967) *Management and Machiavelli*, London: Hodder.

JEFFERY, R. (ed.) (1987) *By What Authority?*, London and Oxford: Mowbray.

KAHN, R.L. and BOULDING, E. (eds) (1964) *Power and Conflict in Organisations*, London: Tavistock.

KANT, I. (1970) *Political Writings*, ed. H. Reiss, trans. H.B. Nisbett, Cambridge: Cambridge University Press.

KATZ, D. and KAHN, R.L. (1966) *The Social Psychology of Organizations*, New York: Wiley.

KAUFMAN, W. (1965) *Hegel*, London: Weidenfeld & Nicolson.

KAUFMAN, W. (1968) *Nietzsche*, Princeton, NJ: Princeton University Press.

KEE, H.C. (1986) *Medicine, Miracle and Magic in New Testament Times*, Cambridge and New York: Cambridge University Press.

KIERKEGAARD, S. (1955) *On Authority and Revelation*, trans. W. Lowrie, Princeton, NJ: Princeton University Press.

KIRSCHT, J.P. and DILLEHAY, R.C. (eds) (1967) *Dimensions of Authoritarianism: A Review of Research and Theory*, Lexington, KY: University of Kentucky Press.

KLEIN, M. *et al.* (1955) *New Directions in Psychoanalysis*, London: Tavistock.

KOESTLER, A. (1964) *The Act of Creation*, London: Hutchinson.

KUHN, T.S. (1970) *The Structure of Scientific Revolutions*, 2nd edn, Chicago: University of Chicago Press.

LAKATOS, I. and MUSGRAVE, A. (eds) (1970) *Criticism and the Growth of Knowledge*, Cambridge and New York: Cambridge University Press.

LASSWELL, H.D. (1949) *Power and Personality*, London: Chapman & Hall/New York: Norton (1948).

LASSWELL, H.D. (1951) 'Psychopathology and Politics' (1930) in *The Political Writings*, Glencoe, IL: Free Press.

LASSWELL, H. and KAPLAN, A. (1952) *Power and Society*, London: Routledge & Kegan Paul/New Haven, CT: Yale University Press.

LEE, S. and STANFORD, P. (1990) *Believing Bishops*, London: Faber.

LEWIS, I.M. (1971) *Ecstatic Religion*, Harmondsworth and New York: Penguin.

LUCKMANN, T. (1983) *Life-World and Social Realities*, London: Heinemann.

LUKES, S. (1974) *Power: A Radical View*, London: Macmillan/Atlantic Highlands, NJ: Humanities Press.

LUTHER, M. (1959) 'Large Catechism', in *The Book of Concord*, ed. T. Tappert, Philadelphia: Fortress Press.

MACCOBY, M. (1981) *The Leader*, New York: Simon & Schuster.

MCDOUGALL, W. (1927) *The Group Mind*, 2nd edn, Cambridge: Cambridge University Press (1920)/Salem, NH: Ayer.

MACHIAVELLI, N. (1961) *The Prince*, trans. G. Bull, Harmondsworth: Penguin.

MACINTYRE, A. (1981) *After Virtue: A Study in Moral Theory*, London: Duckworth/Notre Dame, IN: Notre Dame University Press.

MACQUARRIE, J. (1986) *Theology, Church and Ministry*, London, SCM/New York: Crossroad.

MANNHEIM, K. (1940) *Man and Society in an Age of Reconstruction*, London: Kegan Paul (in German 1935).

MARCUSE, H. (1964) *One Dimensional Man*, London: Routledge & Kegan Paul/Boston: Beacon Press.

MARCUSE, H. (1969) *An Essay on Liberation*, Harmondsworth: Penguin/Boston: Beacon Press.

MARCUSE, H. (1973) 'A Study on Authority' (1936) in *Studies in Critical Philosophy*, Boston: Beacon Press/London: New Left Books (1972).

MEDHURST, K. and MOYSER, G. (1988) *Church and Politics in a*

Secular Age, Oxford and New York: Clarendon Press.

MENZIES, I.I.P. (1970) *The Functioning of Social Systems as a Defence against Anxiety*, London: Tavistock.

MERTON, R.K. (1976) *Sociological Ambivalence and Other Essays*, New York: Free Press.

MILGRAM, S. (1974) *Obedience to Authority: An Experimental View*, London: Tavistock/New York: Harper & Row.

MILL, J.S. (1974) *On Liberty*, Harmondsworth and New York: Penguin.

MILLER, E.J. and RICE A.K. (1967) *Systems of Organization*, London: Tavistock.

MILLER, P. (1987) *Domination and Power*, London: Routledge & Kegan Paul.

MORGAN, G. (1986) *Images of Organisation*, London: Sage.

MOYSER, G. (ed.) (1985) *Church and Politics Today*, Edinburgh: T. & T. Clark/Philadelphia: Fortress.

NEWMAN, J.H. (1833) *Tracts for the Times*, no. 1, Oxford.

NG, S.H. (1980) *The Social Psychology of Power*, London and New York: Academic Press.

PARSONS, T. (1949) *The Structure of Social Action*, 2nd edn, Glencoe: Free Press.

PATON, D.M. (ed.) (1958) *Essays in Anglican Self-Criticism*, London: SCM.

PENNOCK, J.R. and CHAPMAN, J.W. (eds) (1987) *Authority Revisited* (*Nomos* XXIX), New York: New York University Press.

PLATO (1970) *The Laws*, trans. T.J. Saunders, Harmondsworth and New York: Penguin.

POLANYI, M. (1946) *Science, Faith and Society*, Oxford: Oxford University Press/Chicago: University of Chicago Press.

POPPER, K. (1959) *The Logic of Scientific Discovery*, London: Hutchinson/New York: Harper & Row.

POPPER, K. (1963) *Conjectures and Refutations*, London: Routledge & Kegan Paul/New York: Harper & Row.

POPPER, K. (1966) *The Open Society and its Enemies*, 2 vols; 5th edn, London: Routledge & Kegan Paul/Princeton, NJ: Princeton University Press.

RAHNER, K. (1988) *Theological Investigations*, vol. XXI, London:

Darton, Longman & Todd/New York: Crossroad.

REED, B. (1978) *The Dynamics of Religion*, London: Darton, Longman & Todd.

REICH, W. (1975) *The Mass Psychology of Fascism*, Harmondsworth: Penguin/New York: Farrar, Straus & Giroux.

RICE, A.K. (1963) *The Enterprise and its Environment*, London: Tavistock.

RICE, A.K. (1965) *Training for Leadership*, London: Tavistock.

RICOEUR, P. (1986) *Lectures on Ideology and Utopia*, ed. G.H. Taylor, New York: Columbia University Press.

ROBERTSON, R. and HOLZNER, B. (eds) (1980) *Identity and Authority*, Oxford: Basil Blackwell/New York: St Martin's Press.

ROKEACH, M. (1960) *The Open and Closed Mind*, New York: Basic Books.

RUNCIE, R. (1988) *Authority in Crisis: An Anglican Response*, London SCM.

Rural Church Project (1990) D. Davie, M. Winter *et al.*, Nottingham and Cirencester.

RUSSELL, A. (1980) *The Clerical Profession*, London: SPCK.

RUSSELL, B. (1938) *Power: A New Social Analysis*, London: Allen & Unwin/New York: Norton.

SCHLEIERMACHER, F.D.E. (1928) *The Christian Faith*, Edinburgh: T. & T. Clark/Philadelphia: Fortress.

SELZNICK, P. (1966) *Leadership in Administration: A Sociological Interpretation*, New York: Harper (1957).

SHAW, G. (1983) *The Cost of Authority*, London: SCM/Philadelphia: Fortress.

SHÜTZ, J.H. (1975) *Paul and the Anatomy of Apostolic Authority*, Cambridge: Cambridge University Press.

SIMON, H.A. (1955) *Administrative Behavior*, New York: Macmillan (1945).

SIMON, H.A. (1960) *The New Science of Management Decision*, New York: Harper & Row.

SIMON, Y. (1980) *A General Theory of Authority*, Notre Dame, IN: University of Notre Dame Press (1962).

SOFER, C. (1972) *Organisations in Theory and Practice*, London: Heinemann.

SOLIGNAC, P. (1982) *The Christian Neurosis*, London: SCM/New York: Crossroad.

S T O R R, A. (1976) *The Dynamics of Creation*, Harmondsworth and New York: Penguin (1972).

S U P P E, F. (ed.) (1974) *The Structure of Scientific Theories*, Champaign, IL: University of Illinois Press.

S Y K E S, S. W. (1984) *The Identity of Christianity*, London: SPCK/Philadelphia: Fortress.

S Y K E S, S. W. (ed.) (1987) *Authority in the Anglican Communion*, Toronto: Anglican Book Centre.

TDNT Theological Dictionary of the New Testament, Grand Rapids, MI: Eerdmans, 1964–75.

The Nature of Christian Belief, London: Church House, 1986.

T H O M P S O N, K. A. (1970) *Bureaucracy and Church Reform*, Oxford: Clarendon Press.

T O W L E R, R. and C O X O N, A. P. M. (1979) *The Fate of the Anglican Clergy*, London: Macmillan.

V I C K E R S, G. (1965) *The Art of Judgement: A Study of Policy Making*, London: Chapman & Hall/New York: Harper & Row.

V I C K E R S, G. (1973) *Making Institutions Work*, London: Associated Business Programmes.

W A L K E R, A. (1989) *Restoring the Kingdom*, revised edn, London: Hodder.

W A T T, E. D. (1982) *Authority*, Beckenham, Kent: Croom Helm/New York: St Martin's Press.

W E B E R, M. (1964) *The Theory of Social and Economic Organization*, New York: Free Press.

W E I L, S. (1958) *Oppression and Liberty*, London: Routledge & Kegan Paul.

W H I T A K E R, D. S. (1985) *Using Groups to Help People*, London, Routledge & Kegan Paul/New York: Methuen.

W H I T E H E A D, A. N. (1938) *Modes of Thought*, Cambridge: Cambridge University Press/New York: Free Press.

W R O N G, D. H. (1979) *Power: Its Forms, Bases and Uses*, Oxford: Blackwell.

Y O U N G, F. and F O R D, D. F. (1987) *Meaning and Truth in 2 Corinthians*, London: SPCK/Grand Rapids, MI: Eerdmans.

Index of Names and Authors

Abbott, W. M. 5
Acton, Lord 127
Adair, J. 130
Adorno, T. W. 32, 38ff., 41ff., 44, 46, 50f.
Apuleius 79
Arato, A. 43f.
Arendt, H. xii, 26ff., 28f., 35, 87
Argyris, C. 62, 116f.
Augustine of Hippo 79

Bacon, F. 17, 27
Barnard, C. 108, 122
Barr, J. 51f.
Barrett, C. K. 20, 72f.
Barth, K. 89
Benne, K. 115f.
Bennis, W. G. 56f., 98, 112, 116
Bergson, H. 84f.
Berlin, I. 30, 92
Bhaskar, R. 94
Bierstedt, R. 21
Bion, W. R. 110ff., 119, 123
Boff, L. 22
Boulding, E. 119
Brewster Smith, M. 39f.
Brinkman, B. 5
Bunting, I. xii, 102, 104, 108
Butler, R. J. 129

Caillois, R. 67

Calvin, J. 32f.
Caplan, L. 51f.
Chapman, J. W. 124
Churchill, R. S. 16
Churchill, W. S. 16
Clifford, W. K. 47
Cosimo the Old 17
Coxon, A. P. M. 102f.
Croce, B. 17

Dahrendorf, R. 21
de Board, R. 122
de Maistre, J. 59
Descartes, R. 29
Dieckmann, H. 23ff., 45f., 124
Dillehay, R. C. 40
Dostoyevsky, F. 41, 86
Drucker, P. 112
Duncan, H. D. 88
Dunn, J. D. G. 71ff., 77

Eisenstadt, S. N. 68, 70
Emerson, R. W. 95
Emmet, D. 55, 65f.
Erikson, E. 68
Evans, C. F. 77f.

Festinger, L. 40
Feyerabend, P. 91
Foerster, W. 19
Ford, D. F. 125f.

142